KU-513-089

Contents

Introduction

Approaches to Lincoln

Lincoln is a name famous throughout the English-speaking world and beyond. Many people know that the place exists, but little else. 'Where *is* Lincoln exactly?' 'The Lincoln Imps – why is the football team called that?' 'Doesn't it have a lovely cathedral?' 'That's in potato country, isn't it?' The county is also popularly known for its supposedly flat landscapes, its holiday resorts, its pork-based 'delicacies', for its former poaching (wages were low, poverty widespread), and occasional eccentric or misguided political figures. While it is true that Lincoln is not the sort of place that many regularly pass through by road or rail, the general level of ignorance about it, and about the county as a whole, is disconcerting to local people. Although I was raised only 40 miles to the west, we looked to York – a similar distance away – as the great historic town, and Lincoln was always bypassed on our many trips to the Lincolnshire seaside. Few know of the city's associations with the famous, or with famous events. Here are but two: the first tank was tested here, the Samaritans founded.

It is a common place-name in North America – the number of Lincolns, including one state capital, runs into double figures – but they of course were derived from the president (whose ancestors actually lived in Norfolk, England); thus the 'Lincoln' automobile in the USA. In Britain, we have 'Lincoln' biscuits. It is a convenient name to market a product, in both Anglo-Saxon cultures conveying traditional strengths. Perhaps the most historical allusions are to 'Lincoln Green', the cloth worn by Robin Hood and his fellows, and Lincoln College, Oxford, founded by a Bishop of Lincoln. There is also a Lincoln in Australia – Port Lincoln – currently twinned with its English counterpart – and Lincolnshire as a whole has strong historical links with explorers and settlers of former colonies.

My concern is with the original Lincoln. I hope in this short book to convey something of the remarkably rich history of this English

v

Lincoln, and of the delights of experiencing its historic attractions at first hand. The city may never be as popular with visitors as York, but its cultural attractions draw more and more each year. About a quarter of a million take over part of the historic centre in a four-day period for its Christmas Market, the largest event of its kind in Britain. The following pages may help both visitors and Lincolnians alike to take part in a wider appreciation than is possible from a brief tour.

Getting There

Whether travelling by road, rail or water the modern visitor to our city will be aware that arriving in Lincoln is quite unlike arriving anywhere else. Some towns may be just as impressive in their own ways, but no other possesses quite the character of Lincoln's hilltop cathedral and the hill spread below in an otherwise flattish landscape. There is, in other words, a strong 'sense of place'.

Reaching that place is not such a rapid process as for many towns. For several hundred years Lincoln has lain 15 miles or so to the east of principal arteries of communication, so that the traveller undergoes a period of 'depressurization' in the half-hour or so after leaving the A1 or the main East Coast Railway line. I always maintain to outsiders that this is a valuable experience, to encourage them to adjust from the hectic speed of metropolitan life to a pace which, though still fast by pre-industrial standards, might encourage them to take more note of their surroundings. An appreciation of its historic townscape, its topography and its architectural riches is life-enhancing and something which, once developed, is rarely lost. The historic cores of our cathedral cities are pleasing environments, part of the image of itself which England is proud to offer to the world.

The countryside around the city is not the most admired: the poet Robert Southey even commented that it got drearier the nearer he approached. On the other hand, the city itself became more impressive. The most attractive approach to Lincoln is perhaps from the west, via the railway, or from the A57 or the (A46) relief road constructed several years ago, whence the Witham gap and the dominant site of the cathedral can really be appreciated. But other views are equally impressive: those from the south or north offering occasional glimpses of the cathedral's full length, while from either side of Horncastle, 20 miles to the east, the profile of the gap, with the hill crowned by the triple towers, is another delight. Within the city, traffic can move slowly – this is no bad thing – but jams are not often of the same proportions as can regularly be found in other cities of similar attraction.

Sadly for Lincolnians – and after more than twenty years here I count myself as one of them – improvements to local road links seem only to be achieved long after they are patently needed, and while I write Lincoln has lost its only direct train to London. The population of the county is seemingly too low and thinly spread to justify its continuation, but with that fact comes a part of the charm of the area. Rather like the Anglo-Saxon kingdom of Lindsey, ruled successively by Northumbria and by Mercia, present day Lincolnshire is in the catchment area of greater population centres; television comes from Leeds or Nottingham. Lincoln is in any case no stranger to such knocks, nor to criticism, and its people take a philosophical view of events, but are justly proud enough of their city to resent ill-informed critics. As a recent questionnaire has shown, Lincolnians are keen for the city to thrive and develop and feel frustrated that each time they take three steps forward, there can also be two steps back.

Lincoln's magnificent array of monuments has drawn travellers over centuries, and some of them have left accounts of the place. Much of the writing, from the sixteenth-century antiquary John Leland onwards, was concerned with noting and interpreting ancient remains. Others have seen fit to comment, sometimes unfavourably, on the contemporary state of the town. This is particularly true for the seventeenth and early eighteenth centuries, when much of the medieval fabric was in an advanced state of decay. Hence John Evelyn in 1654: 'an old, confus'd town, very long, uneven, steepe, and ragged; formerly full of good houses . . .'; and Abraham de la Pryme (1690): ''Tis a strange thing that great towns should so decay and be eaten up with time . . . there is scarce anything worth seeing in it but the High Street.' Perhaps the most often quoted phrase is that of Daniel Defoe early in the eighteenth century: 'an ancient, ragged, decay'd and still decaying city'. These all preceded the emergence and growth of the modern city during the next two centuries.

Lincoln at the end of the twentieth century has many facets. The hill has created a somewhat misleading picture, for most commercial activity has always taken place 'below hill', nearer to the river. Not only is it an historic cathedral city, but for over a century it has been a centre of heavy engineering, some connected with local agriculture, others of world renown. This industry has witnessed some decline in recent years – as almost everywhere else – but the city has made strenuous and partially successful attempts to attract new industries to the area. These efforts continue, and as I write an announcement about a proposed new university by the Brayford Pool is giving hope

General view of the city looking westwards (towards the Trent Valley)

of a major stimulus over the next decade. Third time lucky, perhaps? University colleges were proposed early this century and again in the early 1960s. Would the city have been a different place?

Unlike most of the rest of Europe, England's most historic cities have not become our major twentieth-century centres, London being the great exception. It was the development of trade and commerce after the medieval period which created Britain's other great population centres, rather than an existing framework. As a result, Lincoln and its ilk preserve much of their medieval feel. The current population of the Lincoln 'District' is about eighty-five thousand; tens of thousands more live within 10 miles. It has good and improving shopping facilities, moderate but improving cultural activity, and occasional major events. The City Council has given strong support to a number of local amenities – the theatre, the football club, and the Archaeology Unit among them.

What sort of town is it? I referred earlier to the 'sense of place': there is more than that, there is a sense of the past. That has much to do with the awesome presence and scale of the cathedral of course, but also with the charm of the complexity of architectural styles and monuments: gates dating from the Roman period, houses dating from the twelfth century and every period since, juxtaposed harmoniously and sometimes enhanced by their location along streets which can be narrow, cobbled and winding. One fact which I hope this book makes plain is that the city contains so much more than the cathedral, spaces and sights which are a joy to discover. Yet between the buildings

The central shopping area on a typically busy day, looking north towards the Stonebow

The top of Steep Hill looking towards Castle Hill

views of the cathedral towers appear regularly as a landmark and a reminder, and for many as a comfort. Those of us who live in and love Lincoln never fail to find pleasure in that landmark either in daylight or floodlit at night when we return from a day or longer away. It was more in relief that the RAF crews flying back from missions in the Second World War recognized the shape of the minster on their return. The RAF is still a major presence in the Lincoln area.

The Urban Village

This pride and delight in the city makes Lincoln a pleasant, congenial place to live and stay. Among the minority who leave, some originating from the city, are those called on to take a more central role in national life, and for this they must depart for the 'big city'. Those who undergo this experience look back with affection on their time in Lincoln. My own experiences may be worth relating here. On arriving in Lincoln at the age of twenty-five, after six years in a northern metropolitan university environment, I found some problems adjusting to the natural reserve of the people and to the way in which provincial society operated. Only later did I realize that all along I had been accepted, and that what I was now a part of was more akin to 'real life' than that of higher education. There are strong contrasts between lifestyles in these two distinct types of urban environment. The big city – and Manchester, which I know best, will serve as an example – is impressive, always buzzing, with a feel that important events are about to happen. Lincoln ticks along more gently, on a longer time-scale, and nothing very big happens very quickly. Its people may appear docile, but they are also shrewd, as some politicians have found to their cost. It is small enough to come across friends and acquaintances frequently about town. I know where I prefer to live, and I hope that it is not just because of the onset of middle age.

Like all towns, Lincoln saw much good architecture – and archaeology below ground – destroyed in modernizing periods up to the early 1970s, to be replaced by buildings whose style has not so far found widespread approval. Wholesale redevelopment and newness were the spirit of that age, but this onslaught naturally provoked a strong reaction. It was even featured in a BBC TV *Chronicle* programme in 1973, in which I was allowed to give my honest opinion of the potential of the Brayford Pool. Conservation has since become the dominant philosophy. I now work in a city whose surviving architectural gems are no longer so vulnerable, and where society's recognition of the importance of preserving and enhancing the city's unique character has been endorsed by planning policies. The basis of planning for the foreseeable future is the 'sustainable' city, reconciling and balancing social, economic and environmental needs.

The Evidence

The early 1970s also witnessed increasing awareness of the need to record archaeological remains at risk from foundations and basements of the new buildings, offices and multi-storey car-parks prominent among them, which appeared in growing numbers from the late 1950s. Lincoln had its share, most built on the lower hillside or close to the river. This is why most archaeological investigations of the 1970s took place in that part of town. Since then there have been considerable developments in archaeological techniques and methods, and more recently a move to preserving buried remains *in situ* rather than allowing them to be removed even through controlled excavation. This new era of preservation provides a useful pause for thought: much of the data obtained from excavation has still to be studied thoroughly, and ideas, approaches and conclusions are constantly being modified.

Archaeology has been mentioned first here because it has been the particular concern of the author, but it is only one type of evidence on which our understanding of Lincoln's historical development is based. It tends to offer us detailed glimpses of small samples of past life, thereby complementing other disciplines, including the study of documents, topographical drawings, place names, architectural history and urban geography. Some of these are also concerned with detail, others with a 'broad brush' picture, and they too have advanced and their results can be integrated into a general synthesis. The city has benefited from sustained work by several distinguished scholars in the above fields, and the research involved in writing this history has been an education for me too. There is an almost limitless wealth of historical interest. For recent history, Lincoln now has an additional band of enthusiastic local historians who have produced a whole host of well-researched volumes on many aspects of city life in the nineteenth and twentieth centuries, on such subjects as industry, railways, the wars, the churches and local institutions. I apologize that this book cannot do justice to them or even refer to them all, but I hope that it will encourage some readers to develop their own interests further.

Deep excavations in progress on Hungate in 1985. At this point on the lower hillside, archaeological deposits can be over 5 m deep

For this recent period, of course, sources are much more plentiful than for the first millennium or so of the city's history, for which we must rely largely on archaeological evidence. Some archaeological remains still survive above ground, but only as the tip of an iceberg. The occupation of the present historic core over two thousand years by communities varying from one hundred to, say, ten thousand in number has created an accumulation of archaeological deposits, produced by the introduction of materials for building, food, and other purposes. In places, these deposits are 5 m deep, elsewhere they can be very shallow: on average, the modern surface is about 3 m above that of the original site, but the whole problem is compounded by the difficult topography of the hillside, and the resultant need to terrace. We can say that what survives is only the tiniest fraction of what once existed. The archaeologist thus has the smallest of samples on which to base arguments: this is partly why we need to carry out more research if we are to understand what really happened.

For the 350 years of the Roman period alone, the first major era in the city's history, roughly between fifty and a hundred thousand people must have lived and died here. Few of their mortal remains now lie intact in their graves, because of the actions of subsequent generations. One can also estimate that, since its foundation, the city has had between half a million and a million citizens, approximately half of whom lived only after the onset of the Industrial Revolution. This book is dedicated to those Lincolnians past and present, and to their descendants.

Among past citizens mentioned there will, in any historical work, be a bias in favour of the rich and powerful. Yet the poor, and the fate of ordinary people – often unknown – are regular themes. I have tried to aim for a balance between what life was like for the privileged and conditions for the majority, always fairly wretched, often exploited. Other themes, such as the contrast between uphill society and downhill commerce and industry, recur regularly. Growth is often equated in earlier history with exclusively positive benefits, and of course it should be if it alleviated misery. But our environmentally aware generation may have a different perspective. Moreover it is healthy to be open about conflicts both in society and in their historical interpretation. I have also tried to provide a general narrative, but for a city whose history (as set out by Sir Francis Hill) has already occupied four substantial volumes, it has been necessary in such a brief volume to be selective. I have therefore included facts and features which I consider to be of most interest to those for whom this represents an introduction. I hope that it will be only the start of their learning to appreciate the historical wealth of a town too little known and known by too few.

CHAPTER ONE

Romans and Countrymen

Origins

T he Jurassic Ridge running north–south through Lincolnshire formed the basis for an early routeway (a 'Jurassic Walk'!), which clung close to its western scarp (the 'Lincoln Edge'). Thousands of years ago, glacial action carved a hole through this ridge: the resultant gap, about a mile wide, is now occupied by the River Witham and its attendant marshes, at the point where it meets the River Till flowing from the west. At the meeting of the rivers a lake formed, now known as the Brayford Pool.

Geology and topography of the Lincoln area showing late prehistoric and later water courses and prehistoric features east of the city

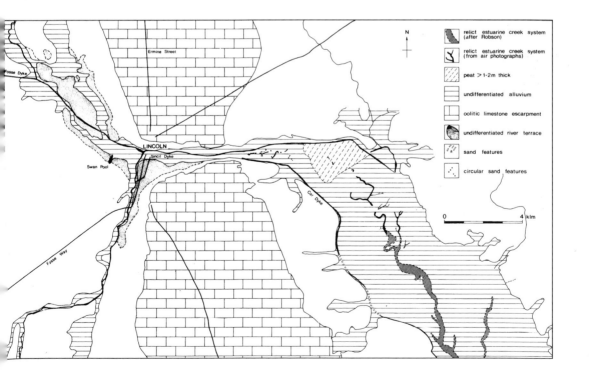

N

relict estuarine creek system (after Robson)

relict estuarine creek system (from air photographs)

peat > 1-2m thick

undifferentiated alluvium

oolitic limestone escarpment

undifferentiated river terrace

sand features

circular sand features

Ermine Street

Fosse Dyke

LINCOLN

Sincil Dyke

Swan Pool

Car Dyke

Fosse Way

0   4 k|m

The combination of routeway and river formed a natural site for settlement. In due course, its strategic importance was realized by the Roman army, but our earliest evidence for settlement belongs to the first century BC. Excavations in 1972 to the east of Brayford Pool revealed slight traces of timber houses and contemporary pottery, on a knoll of higher, drier ground. This was an unexpected discovery; but should it have been? The first syllable of the Roman name *Lindum* is derived from the Celtic word for 'pool' or 'lake'. How extensive this settlement was we may never know: its remains lie deeply buried beneath the heart of the modern shopping area.

But these were not the first prehistoric finds from Lincoln, and the few miles to its east, where the valley is at its narrowest, and crossing least difficult, have been the most productive. Dredging of the Witham has brought to light some remarkable treasures, some dating to the third and second centuries BC, the most famous being the Witham Shield. Now in the British Museum (a replica can be seen in Lincoln), the shield is an excellent example of 'Celtic' art, with clear European influence in the style of its decoration. The wealth of the local chieftains was probably based on farming and on salt obtained from the coast – then nearer to Lincoln than now. The tribe covering the area of Lincolnshire and much of the East Midlands was probably called the 'Corieltauvi'. They had some large open settlements, and coinage and pottery both linked in style to that of the 'Kentish' tribes. Their principal centres appear to have lain at Leicester and at old Sleaford, almost 20 miles south of Lincoln.

The Witham Shield (British Museum)

The Roman Arrival

During the middle of the first century AD the native settlers were moved from their site. Whether they were friendly or hostile to the Roman army of conquest we do not know, but it is clear that the Ninth Legion took over a large area for its own purposes. It too saw the occupation of the gap as essential, on the route of conquest northwards, a river crossing to be defended, and perhaps both to block unfriendly east–west movement and also to use the river for its own supply purposes. Evidence for the legion was found last century in the form of several tombstones, including that of the standard bearer, Caius Valerius. There were also two tombstones of Legio II Adiutrix, which replaced the Ninth in AD 71.

Most of the tombstones were found in the lower part of the town, which might indicate an early fortress in that area. The fact of their lacking surnames (*cognomina*) might suggest a date during the reign

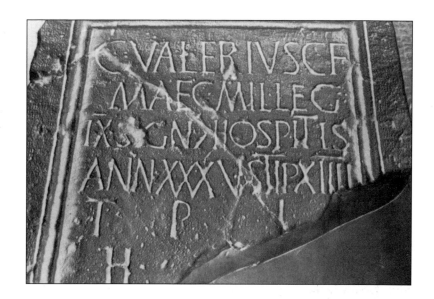

Tombstone of Caius Valerius, standard bearer of the Ninth Legion

Artist's reconstruction of the hilltop Roman legionary fortress (D.R. Vale)

of Claudius (AD 41–54). But the fortress whose existence beneath the later Roman city was established in the 1940s appears to date from the time of Nero (AD 54–65), and some authors have argued for a foundation date of AD 61 following the suppression of the rebellion of Boudicca. Further archaeological research may produce more precise dating than we have at present.

Several excavations confirmed that the fortifications of the legionary fortress lay directly beneath those of the *colonia*. An earthen bank was held in place by timbers front and rear, and fronted by a V-shaped ditch. Little is known of the interior: strong conservation policies make it unlikely that much more will ever be known. But we have a few glimpses, of parts of timber barrack blocks, and in particular of the legionary headquarters, the *principia*. Excavation work in 1978–9 revealed the north-west corner of its courtyard, defined by a verandah, with the main aisled hall, or *basilica*, to its west. This arrangement confirmed that the fortress had faced eastwards.

Although some modifications took place, possibly at the time the legions changed, it was never rebuilt in stone: its occupation was not to last more than twenty to thirty years, by the end of which the tribal area of the Corieltauvi was considered to be sufficiently pacified for the military zone to be moved northwards and westwards. The Ninth went on to build York, the Second Adiutrix Chester. Nevertheless, the presence of a legion of about five thousand soldiers necessitated a communications infrastructure including major roads from the south and south-west, the Ermine Street (now partly the A15) and the Fosse Way (now the A46). Moreover, it attracted a community of traders and other natives who were largely dependent on the legionaries' spending power and essential needs. The site of the fortress could be maintained and developed as a civil settlement, without too much further disruption of local property rights.

Colony

As at Colchester before and Gloucester shortly afterwards, the decision was taken to dismantle the fortress structures and to create on their site a *colonia*, a prestigious self-governing community of time-served legionaries. On retirement, the soldiers were given grants of money and land, the latter to enable them to create wealth which could in due course be spent on developing their city on the Roman model. No doubt there were veterans of several legions, including the Ninth, as well as native settlers. The exact date at which *Lindum Colonia* came into existence is uncertain: a dedication stone in the museum at Mainz in Germany shows that it was before AD 96; it is unlikely to have taken place before the Scottish campaigns of the mid-80s came to an end.

The new city witnessed a major programme of public works over the next few decades. The fortifications were provided with a stone wall at their front, embellished by a series of towers at intervals of approximately 50 m, and a new outer ditch. The spiritual and physical centre of the new city was the forum. This was erected on the site of its natural predecessor, the *principia*, but, unlike that at Gloucester, did not simply follow the same plan. In its first manifestation, it appears to have included an open precinct containing some official statues. Subsequently, the town hall or *basilica* was erected on the north side of the courtyard, which was otherwise surrounded by double ranges of rooms. Porticoed walkways overlooked the central piazza, and a magnificent colonnade including two entrances provided an impressive frontage on to the main street of the city. The style of the forum at Lincoln seems to be more continental in design than most in Roman Britain: among its earliest citizens would have been ex-soldiers of Mediterranean origins, and as a *colonia* it was encouraged to be an imperial showpiece.

Part of the excavated east range is on display, as is the nearby 'Mint Wall', a section of the north wall of the civic basilica still

Discovery of part of the colonnade of the forum on Bailgate in the late nineteenth century

standing 5 m high. But there is little else remaining above ground of the once-magnificent Roman city. The public baths lay to the north and east of the principal street. There must also have been temples and a theatre, still awaiting discovery. Much of the area away from the centre would have been occupied by well-appointed houses, and chance finds of mosaics and hypocausts (underfloor heating systems) have been noted over recent centuries, but we know little of their plans from modern investigation.

The new colony – formally *Colonia Lindensium*, but usually referred to as *Lindum Colonia*, or simply *Lindum* – was provided with an impressive system of waterworks. Its aqueduct, tapping a source about 2 km to the north-east, may be the most famous in Roman Britain, but its workings are still imperfectly understood, for no-one has satisfactorily explained how water was brought up about 20 m from the spring known as the Roaring Meg to the city. A water-lifting device seems most likely. A tank lined with *opus signinum* (hydraulic cement) which lay behind the north wall may

Artist's reconstruction of the upper Roman city looking south-west, with the forum and basilica in the centre, and postulated temple to the south. The public baths are also shown on the left (D.R. Vale)

have served as a reservoir: its position is marked out on a site north of East Bight, adjacent to a stretch of city wall. From here the water would have supplied the baths and helped to flush out the sewers, which are known beneath several streets: again the evidence from Lincoln is of national renown.

This impression of a city blessed with major engineering works for public facilities is a real one, and was further enhanced during the later second and early third centuries by more developments. They included the rebuilding of some of the gates with impressive towers: evidence can still be seen at the east and north gates. But it is a one-sided picture, because commercial activity was from the start an essential element of the life of the town. Shops are known across the street from the baths, and were presumably provided in the forum complex, but were to be found in greater number outside the walls of the colonia.

The hillside below the fortress was probably occupied by commercial traders from the late first century. Later it seems that these south facing slopes were largely given over to residential use, apart from the main street itself which contained several public buildings and a fountain. The settlement as far as the river was subsequently included within the fortified area, an operation which appears to have taken almost a century to complete and to have consumed a substantial part of the civic purse.

There was also extensive development beyond. The riverside must have been a bustling focus of trading activity – river transportation

Plan of the walled Roman city

A Roman balance and some of the coins found well preserved in excavations at Waterside North, 1988

cost only a fraction of that by road – but excavations have so far only revealed glimpses. Beneath the new Waterside Shopping Centre, work in 1987–90 revealed a series of inlets and artificial piers. Those excavations produced vast amounts of well-preserved artefacts, including large numbers of leather shoes and part of a Roman writing-tablet. There were dumps of butcher's waste, which will aid our understanding of the local diet; and one sample of the waterlogged earth contained forty-seven species of plant, which is throwing light on the local environment, crops grown and weeds present, as well as confirming earlier evidence that the river was of moderate flow and almost totally free of tidal influence. The river in the Roman period was much wider, and gradual reclamation was necessary partly because its level was rising but also to create shelving beaches on which to draw up river craft. The only possible evidence for a vertical quay was found in 1954 to the east of Broadgate, just downstream of the walled area. With the construction of the Foss Dyke canal linking the Brayford Pool with the Trent at Torksey, goods could be moved by river between Lincoln and York and by sea to the frontier.

Beyond the river and to the south lay the most extensive suburbs, largely taken up with commercial properties, developed from the second century. These are now known to have extended to about a kilometre to the south of the river, and have been traced on seven different excavation sites. Landfill operations were necessary to secure a sound building level. They were followed by the construction of long narrow buildings, closely set, which had had shops on their street frontages. They must have supplied a variety of products, from foodstuffs to metalwork, to the local populace, but evidence for actual trades is hard to find. Similar properties have also been found outside other gates of the city, while the cemeteries lay in other extra-mural locations along streets. Further out were industrial concerns which supplied the city, including gravel workings, quarries and pottery kilns.

Roman Lincoln was then both a prosperous and populous place. Its population cannot be estimated precisely, but probably numbered between five and ten thousand. Its citizens included some of influence, power and exotic origins, and with 'cultured' taste in the Roman manner. That much is clear from finds of high quality classical sculpture and from a number of tombstones. These include Flavius Helius, a Greek; Claudia Crysis, a nonagenarian (is she the oldest documented person in Roman Britain?), and Volusia Faustina, the wife of Aurelius Senecio, a 'decurion', or city councillor. From

Bordeaux, where he erected an altar, we know of Marcus Aurelius Lunaris, a presumed wine merchant who was also the *sevir augustalis*, priest of the cult of the emperor, at both Lincoln and York.

The Fourth Century

The place of Lincoln on the international map, and its evident prosperity, were perhaps both factors which led to its choice at the end of the third century as a provincial capital, when Britain was subdivided into four. Lincoln became the administrative centre of the new province of Flavia Caesariensis. It was probably its new status which in turn led to its becoming a metropolitan bishopric from 313, sending a delegate, Bishop Adelfius, to the first Christian Council in the west, held at Arles in southern Gaul in the following year. The presence of the new officials in the city meant an injection of spending power and some employment for local people. Moreover, the need to protect this node in the imperial system necessitated a refurbishment of the fortifications, and the extra security thus provided was a further factor in Lincoln's fourth-century prosperity.

The city wall was thickened internally or completely rebuilt to a thickness of 3 to 4 m, and raised to a height of 6 to 7 m. Although the style of the new walls was conservative, a much larger ditch was now created, about 25 m wide, in keeping with late Roman defensive strategy. It is difficult to underestimate the scale of this undertaking, which may have commenced before the end of the third century and was still in process after 350. It served to create a defensive barrier which survived for several centuries and influenced the layout of the town for even longer. The later Roman work included two new gates in the lower circuit, one a postern leading to the riverside, the other of uncertain purpose. Both included reused fragments from earlier monuments, reminders of a more optimistic era.

The early fourth century was also the period when the city and its suburbs were at their greatest extent. Money was still being lavished on aristocratic town houses – the local elite were investing in their rural villas too – but little in the way of public building was taking place apart from that on the city walls. In effect, those with the resources were less prepared to invest in public works; there was rather a 'privatization' of ostentatious expenditure, a symptom perhaps of a changing economy and society.

Excavations suggest that, in spite of a possible decline in public amenities, occupation of the city continued at a considerable level well into the second half of the century. Houses, shops, the riverside, and public buildings all show signs of activity until *c.* 375–80. Moreover the major pottery industry of Swanpool to the south-west of the city was still vibrant to the same period, producing principally for the local market. Although our dating evidence for the period after 380 becomes difficult, it is apparent that all parts of the town still contained residents to the end of the century. And yet there is clear evidence of a gradual reduction and abandonment.

While some parts of the town were clearly still being used and money exchanged into the next century, much of the former town became blanketed with a layer of what archaeologists term 'dark earth'. The interpretation of this material, which occurs at many late Roman towns, has never been satisfactorily achieved. In the first instance it is not precisely dateable. Second, its function may have varied from site to site – in some cases it was dumped, in others it accumulated – and analyses which might explain it are still at an early stage. What it does represent is extensive – but not complete – desertion of the urban area, and this in turn might point to a radical change in the economic basis of the settlement. It might well indicate a return to a small self-sufficient community practising agriculture and horticulture and keeping animals within the walls.

The relationship of the physical and economic changes to the organized Church is uncertain. There is, in any case, no consensus about the extent to which Christianity penetrated into the Romano-British population, for the evidence for the British episcopacy in the late fourth century is negligible. It is still quite possible, however, that a considerable band of communicants existed, or at least worshipped, in the city by 400. The site of the bishop's church and residence have not yet been positively identified, although at least one candidate is worthy of consideration: a timber church built in the forum courtyard and later built on a larger scale. In much of Britain, the Roman bishopric, traditionally based in the major towns, survived for several decades, at least, into the fifth century. A small Christian community surviving in and around the town thus provides the likeliest thread of continuity into Lincoln's next epoch: its 'dark ages'.

CHAPTER TWO

Britons, Anglo-Saxons and Danes: *c.* 450–1066

B y the mid-fifth century the area of the formerly prosperous Roman city was more or less deserted, a casualty of the collapse of the Imperial system. Production on a large scale and international trade ceased as the province of Britain was handed over to its own fate. So the Roman system was in terminal decline before the Germanic settlers from across the North Sea appeared in any number, and Lincoln's urban functions had come to an end before the Anglo-Saxon takeover of eastern England. These new settlers brought with them a building tradition in timber, a pagan religion, and a society and an economy in which towns on the Roman model had no place.

By the time of the Norman Conquest six centuries later, Lincoln was again one of England's leading centres. The story of those centuries is not one that can easily be written. Historical sources are few and far between and cannot be taken at face value. Yet this is also the period for which archaeological research has made the greatest recent advances in terms of our understanding of urban origins, and Lincoln itself has produced some notable discoveries. As is often the way, the new finds beg further questions, and our knowledge remains imperfect. We must to some extent therefore rely on analogous evidence from other towns, including some in mainland Europe.

The Pre-Scandinavian Period

The Roman legacy was a solid fortification of approximately 40 hectares (100 acres), with good road and river communications. The former streets went out of use, sooner or later, and most buildings became ruinous, although some survived. Such ruins must have put constraints on small-scale construction schemes and on farming activities. It yet seems probable that a small community continued to occupy the former site of the Roman city, based on an essentially agricultural economy. Although we cannot yet positively identify evidence for agriculture or horticulture in Dark Age Lincoln, these are the most likely land uses, based on evidence from elsewhere in Britain and Northern Europe. For instance, recent excavations near the cathedral at Rouen in Normandy have discovered traces of pits containing compost within 'dark earth' layers of the fifth to seventh centuries.

We know little of the kingdom of Lindsey ('the island of the people of Lincoln'), which emerged by the end of the sixth century, because it was always in the second rank politically. But archaeology is of some help. Analysis of pottery from excavations has identified a few sherds of pagan Saxon date (i.e. before *c.* 650), but not easily capable of more precise dating. The Anglo-Saxons did at some stage take political control of the site. Bede wrote of the events of *c.* 627–8 when Bishop Paulinus came to Lincoln from York, and was met by a man called Blecca, described as *praefectus civitatis* – 'prefect of the city' (this title can be taken to imply someone of considerable political importance, if not the king of Lindsey then the nearest thing). Paulinus converted Blecca and his household, and then went on to build a stone church 'of remarkable workmanship'. Bede also reports that the church was used for the consecration of Honorius, the fifth Archbishop of Canterbury, a service carried out by Paulinus. By Bede's time (a century later), however, it lay ruinous.

Who exactly were these people, and how did they relate to the survivors of the Roman period? Here the evidence from the former Roman forum site is central to our understanding: but it is difficult evidence, and capable of several interpretations. The structures include a succession of two timber churches, built on the forum courtyard and related architecturally to the western portico of the forum. Slight dating evidence from pottery and coins indicate that they were built no earlier than the fourth century, while radiocarbon analysis of subsequent graves suggests that the second, larger, church had probably been demolished by 600. Because of their timber construction method and their probable date they cannot easily be equated with the church built by Paulinus.

There are two other possible contexts. One would involve the existence of an 'episcopal group' – one or two churches, baptistery (the well in the forum east range?), and palace – serving the late Roman bishop. Such a phenomenon is common in Gaul but not yet definitely known from Britain. It would not be expected to appear in any case before the end of the fourth century. And yet it is still possible that a small, 'sub-Roman' Christian community continued with the bishop as its spiritual and political leader for several decades into the fifth century.

Another interpretation would see a British 'tyrannus', a new, self-appointed local leader, establish a power base inside the Roman walls. Re-use of the Roman site would have been partly symbolic, a legitimation of the new ruler's power. The former political centre – the forum and basilica – would house this palace' and the church might serve as the 'palace-chapel'. In due course, and by intermarriage or pressure rather than open hostility, the British hegemony would be ceded to Anglo-Saxons. Implicit in this idea is the assumption that Lincoln was or became the major, if not the only, political centre in Lindsey, though lying on its southern boundary. Interestingly, a genealogy of the Lindsey kings includes one 'Caedbad', a Celtic name. So Lincoln may have remained for a while a separate entity, before being swallowed up by forces from the north. It may have subsequently superseded an earlier capital: reference in 803 to the Bishop of *Syddensis civitas*, if a misrendering for the 'southern city', may mean Lincoln, either as the more southerly of two main political centres of the kingdom, or in relation to York. A location at Lincoln would in any case be more appropriate by then, for Lindsey had become part of the Mercian Empire and thus had closer links with lands south of the Witham.

The above hypotheses represent informed speculations about what *might* have happened. Apart from the evidence of the churches on the forum site – later the church of St-Paul-in-the-Bail – archaeology has revealed negligible traces of occupation between the fourth and late ninth centuries. It is difficult to know if burial, perhaps restricted to an 'aristocratic' group, continued without a break within the former forum courtyard. At some date in the seventh to ninth centuries, an important grave was dug, placed from the start or subsequently within a rectangular mausoleum or chapel. On discovery in 1978 it was found that any human remains had been removed in antiquity, perhaps 'translated' to a more appropriate site such as a minster church. Inadvertently, a bronze hanging-bowl deposited in the corner of the grave had been left in position. The bowl has some fine decorative attachments, excellent examples of contemporary Celtic craftsmanship. It remains one of the most exciting finds from the city, dating to the seventh century but of uncertain function. It can be seen in the cathedral treasury, while

Seventh-century bronze hanging bowl found in a special grave at the site of St-Paul-in-the-Bail

Artist's impression of the lower walled town in the eighth century, showing St Peter's church and the diagonal street linking the south and east gates (Silver Street) (D.R. Vale)

some remains of the forum and early church of St-Paul-in-the-Bail have also been laid out for public view.

The single-celled structure containing the grave here subsequently became the original core of a parish church which survived, after many rebuildings, until 1971. The Anglo-Saxon settlement may also have contained a number of other Christian foci. We have not yet found the site of Paulinus' church. If not in the forum area it may have been located just inside the lower walled town north of the Stonebow, where early graves were discovered in 1973 on Silver Street, east of the site of St Peter at Arches. Nearby to the north was another St Peter's church: it is conceivable that they originated from the ruins of the aisles of a great early church. There are reasonable arguments for other early church sites at St Mary le Wigford (by the railway level crossing), at St Martin's (top of High Street), and at All Saints in the Bail (north of Eastgate). It has been argued that the eighth-century bishop had two churches, at least one of them in Lincoln. No archaeological research has yet been possible to investigate these ideas.

Nor has Lincoln produced evidence for an eighth-century riverside trading settlement outside the Roman walls (a 'wic'), as has now emerged at several other towns. Perhaps it is simply not to be found, but more areas of the town would require examination before we could dismiss it as a possibility. More likely, the area contained a number of small farmsteads – one probable location is that indicated by finds of ninth-century pottery in the grounds of The Lawn, west of the castle. New lanes, in some cases short cuts, cutting diagonally over the Roman grid and linking the former Roman gates, must have appeared at about this time. They include Chapel Lane in the upper city and Silver Street in the lower. By the ninth century, coin finds in Lindsey suggest increasing wealth; a group of coins of the early 870s might be seen in this light, as a dispersed hoard. But why was it lost? That wealth was increasingly at risk by raiders from across the sea.

Coin of King Alfred of the 'lunette' series, AD 871–5, found at St-Paul-in-the-Bail

The Danish Commercial Impetus

Lincoln was first seriously affected by the Viking raids in the late ninth century, during the movement of the 'Great Army' through eastern England in the 860s and '70s. In 873 the army wintered at Torksey on the Trent, 12 miles west of Lincoln and at the point where the Foss Dyke canal meets the Trent. They caused much havoc before they met serious resistance from Wessex, and ultimately concluded an agreement in 886 on the extent of their territory – the 'Danelaw'. Before the end of the century Danish settlement had begun and Lincoln became one, and possibly the largest, of the 'Five Boroughs' of the East Midlands; together with Derby, Nottingham, Leicester and Stamford. All of these became 'shires' – areas settled or governed by the armies based in the boroughs – except Stamford, whose shire was incorporated into that of Lincoln.

No doubt the well-preserved Roman fortified circuit and the water communications had proved an attraction to the invading army and in due course they were a factor in the development of the settlement. Recent archaeological research suggests that York and Lincoln grew as quickly as any town in England during the tenth century, and Danish trading activity probably contributed significantly to this growth. Not all the inhabitants of the burgeoning town were Scandinavians, however – the names of the moneyers of the Lincoln mint include as many English as incomers: 'the Danish Grimcetel coined along with the English Godric', as Sir Francis Hill put it.

Some finds of this date were already known from the area of the city, but only within the past twenty years have archaeological techniques been refined and excavations large enough to identify coherent traces of occupation. Now we have sufficient evidence and dating material – in particular helped by detailed study of changing pottery styles – to articulate the general pattern of growth across the city in the two centuries from *c.* 880. One might assume that the principal street frontage was the first to be built up, but that idea cannot yet be supported by hard evidence. The most productive site was that on the corner of Flaxengate and Grantham Street, in the eastern part of the lower walled city. Only this south-eastern quadrant, which contained the churches of St Swithin and St Edmund the King, appears to show much occupation before c. 900. It was soon followed by ribbon development in the southern suburb of Wigford, beyond the river crossing. Perhaps stimulus to settlement in this area was provided by the trading focus of the riverside; alternatively, Wigford might owe its origin, or rather its revival, to Edward the Elder's policy of creating burghs after expelling Viking armies in 918. It may also be at this date that the Sincil Dyke was cut to the east of High Street to help drainage from properties on the street in the same way as the river did to the west. Coin finds of Scandinavian kings occur again in the next two decades, suggesting that control returned temporarily to the Danes. Only later in the tenth century is there evidence that the upper city, perhaps until then a royal preserve, was being penetrated by new settlers. But this observation is based on only limited investigation. Further parts of the lower city and the eastern suburb of Butwerk also seem to have been occupied before the Norman Conquest, but not until the eleventh century.

This south-western part of the lower city would repay further archaeological attention, not only to establish the date of reoccupation but also to identify the site of the Lincoln Mint. Pennies of St Martin appear in the early 920s, modelled on those of St Peter at York. The mint was a major producer of coins from at least the mid-tenth century, and its products are found not only in Lincoln and the locality but also elsewhere in England as well as in Scandinavia. The sheer number of moneyers – over ninety – indicates that it vied in importance with York for second place after London.

Excavations have also revealed a number of silver pennies from other mints, which indicates trading contacts with both England and Scandinavia. Other finds constitute corroborative evidence for that trade and also with north-western Europe. Many of these objects were recovered from the Flaxengate site, which contained remains of both houses and workshops and was probably an industrial quarter. Traces of the timber structures were slight, but enough survived to suggest a whole sequence of about thirteen periods of construction between c. 880 and c. 1230, when the first stone building was erected here – an average life of about twenty-five years. A gradual increase in the sophistication of building methods was discernible. Some at least had rush and sand floors. Most of the walls were probably of horizontally laid planks, their roofs of thatch. There was nothing particularly Scandinavian about these methods of construction, but finds noted above surely confirm the identification of the earlier occupants of the site.

Of considerable importance was the evidence for a new street (Danish 'gata', later our 'gate') laid out in *c*. 900, parallel to the Roman Ermine Street about 200 m to the west: probably the first deliberate act of town planning since the second century. Subsequently an east–west street was constructed to link the two. Workshops and nearby rubbish layers and pits contained many fragments of evidence for industrial activity. Spinning was normally carried out on a domestic scale. Artefacts were being fashioned from bone and antler, including some combs as well as simpler pieces such as pins. Crucible and mould fragments point to metallurgical activity. Many personal ornaments, such as finger rings, were made of glass and copper alloy, some from re-using Roman objects, and from jet, silver and possibly from amber. These all represent a common range of material found on major urban sites of the late Saxon period. The finds also indicate that Lincoln served as a market for the surrounding region; goods were not only being made but also imported for sale in exchange for agricultural produce. There were other local manufactures: at nearby Silver Street production of pottery tempered with fragments of shell began in the late ninth century – three large open kilns were discovered there in 1973. The dry site conditions, however, mean that no organic material survived. We therefore lack a substantial proportion of contemporary material culture, and this imbalance was only partially redressed by finds from Waterside North in 1987–90. Shoes and other leather artefacts, and some wooden objects, were recovered together with microscopic evidence for diet and for the local environment. A rare silk scarf of Byzantine origin turned up at Silver Street, similar enough to be part of the same roll also used for a scarf found in York several years later! Among the seeds were some of bog myrtle, which is known to have been used for brewing ale.

Traces of contemporary domestic occupation have now appeared at several other sites in the city. Such sites can only reveal their secrets, as at Flaxengate, by painstaking excavation and subsequent examination of minute fragments of material, including many scraps of corroded ironwork. Only through such methods can we do justice to these difficult but important remains. A tenth-century coin-die,

Artist's impression of the Brayford waterfront in the eleventh century (R. Sutton)

whose identification was not achieved until more than ten years after its excavation, is a case in point. It is one of only five late Saxon dies found so far in this country.

There were several other areas of pre-Conquest activity in the town, and they too are adding to the picture. In the tenth century a new waterfront was being constructed on the north side of the river. This was a timber structure designed for small rivercraft; part of a hull of a clinker-built boat was incorporated into a later wharf or jetty. Similar, shelving beaches have been noted on the east side of Brayford Pool, and it may have been before the Norman Conquest that the adjacent frontage was exploited for trapping and farming fish.

Parish Origins

While several churches may have existed in the pre-Viking town, the initial impact of Viking raids on Christian places of worship could be devastating. To avoid such damage, the see had been transferred to Dorchester on Thames, south of Oxford, just about the most distant part of this huge diocese from the North Sea. Yet it is apparent that tenth-century Lincoln soon showed many signs of flourishing Christian worship. The emergence of the St Martin penny might reflect the importance of that church, which stood at the point where the upper High Street diverges into two: the medieval lanes here do not follow their Roman predecessor directly up the hill. The possible early establishment of the two St Peter's churches was noted above, while to the east St Swithin and St Edmund the King are likely to have originated in the late ninth or early tenth century. Others have argued for an early Minster of St Mary beneath or near to the present cathedral, but not all scholars are convinced that one existed.

What is clear is that the church of St-Paul-in-the-Bail, so significant for early Christianity in the city, now reverted to the status of an ordinary parish church. Beginning from the single cell already existing, it was enlarged in several stages. The only other church to have been completely excavated is that of St Mark in Wigford. This too appears to have originated in about the mid-tenth century as a small timber structure with an adjacent graveyard. It was later rebuilt in stone on a slightly different site. There was an impressive collection of contemporary tombstones from the early graveyard, some of them built into later foundations. Not only do they suggest some wealth among the parishioners, they also reflect a variety of artistic influence in their decorative style, varying from local and East Anglian to Northumbrian.

The medieval city had nearly fifty parish churches. Documents and architectural evidence indicate that at least thirty-two were in existence by 1100. Archaeology has now extended the origin of parish creation a further century back in time. The most likely context for this process would be as 'proprietary' churches, built by the local landowner, as his property on his land, for the use of his tenants.

By 1066, then, Lincoln was again a busy, bustling, and no doubt dirty, town, still growing, and with churches being built as well as domestic and commercial establishments. The Domesday survey suggests a population of perhaps six to eight thousand, which would put it in the second division after London, with places like Norwich, Winchester and York. The Viking legacy had included some form of local government, in the form of the twelve 'lawmen', the predecessor of the medieval council. They met at the mootstone by St Peter's church. The upper city may have ceased to be a royal preserve, for many houses were there by 1066, but the lower town functioned as the municipal and commercial centre. The domestic building tradition was in timber, and Lincoln contained little in the way of notable monuments apart from decaying Roman structures, notably the city walls: in this sense it lacked a major physical aspect of the Roman city. Yet it was prosperous, a factor which attracted a new group of invaders who were to change the face of Lincoln.

Early church sites in the city

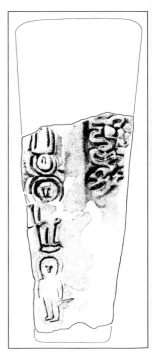

Figured gravestone from St Mark's: late tenth or early eleventh century

CHAPTER THREE

The Medieval Zenith: Castle and Cathedral

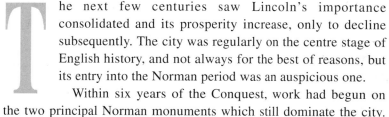

The next few centuries saw Lincoln's importance consolidated and its prosperity increase, only to decline subsequently. The city was regularly on the centre stage of English history, and not always for the best of reasons, but its entry into the Norman period was an auspicious one.

Within six years of the Conquest, work had begun on the two principal Norman monuments which still dominate the city. King Harold, who was killed at Hastings in 1066, was among those who had owned a house in the busy town of Lincoln. His Norman conqueror returned southwards via Lincoln after his first campaign in the north, and ordered a castle to be built. The site chosen by William was the south-western quarter of the upper Roman city, over part of whose west and south walls the earthen bank was raised. It stood up to 9 m high and was in places 25 m wide. Recent investigations connected with ensuring the long-term stabilization of the castle ramparts have suggested that an original bank was first created – this may originally have been topped by a timber palisade. Then the stone wall which would have replaced the palisade was built hand in hand with the rest of the bank. The external ditch was also substantial, but the ground conditions are such that it was never intended to be filled with water.

Coin of William I, of 1072–4, minted at Thetford; found during excavations at St Mark's church

The Domesday survey of 1086 tells us that 166 houses had to be demolished to make way for the castle, which covered almost 14 acres. This was equivalent to about a third of the area of the upper city, though the presence of churches and surviving deeds relating to the area to the north and east may mean that these were not so packed with houses. About a third of the city's population is thought to have dwelt uphill at the time.

The rest of the upper Roman enclosure became the castle's outer bailey – the Bail – and, like the Cathedral Close, did not legally

become part of the city proper again until 1836. Courts and markets uphill were not held by the city but by the castle constable, a position which soon passed to the de la Haye family, one of the many Norman aristocrats to benefit from the new rulers.

Aerial view of the castle and cathedral from the east

William had resorted to the policy of favouring his countrymen partly because the English had not welcomed him with open arms. Lincoln Castle, built largely by resentful local labour, was used initially to imprison hostages from Lindsey. It suffered a fire in 1115, and was later the scene of three military operations of diminishing length. The first took place in 1141 during the dispute between supporters of Stephen and those of his cousin, the Empress Matilda, who was championed by Ranulf, Earl of Chester. The castle changed hands several times before the battle, after which Stephen was imprisoned, and although the attack which he launched in 1144 was unsuccessful, he was back in control again by Christmas 1146. This time, Ranulph was on the side of the king. Another struggle followed in 1216 after the then constable, Nicholaa de la Haye,

Artist's impression of the castle and cathedral from the west, *c.* 1180 (D.R. Vale)

Interior of the Victorian prison chapel at the castle

would not cede the castle to supporters of Louis of France, but the king's army recaptured the city in the following year, before pillaging the town for having supported the opposition. The only other military action which the castle saw was in the Civil War, when Parliamentary troops had little difficulty in storming it. A survey as long before as 1327 had declared it incapable of defence and requiring the sort of investment which was not considered worthwhile at that time of financial difficulty. Some of the internal buildings were also ruinous. Subsequently Charles I sold off the ditches to raise money, and as a result the castle walls are only fully visible where recent clearance has been possible.

The second major phase of the castle's life was then confined to its role as a seat of local government, and of law and order. A new prison was built in 1787–91 after a report emphasized the awfulness of existing conditions. It mainly housed debtors. An extension to the rear in the 1840s was for felons. The new philosophy was the 'Pentonville' system of solitary confinement. Although the prison was closed in 1878 the building still displays its unique prison chapel and now contains a new exhibition about Magna Carta. The nearby Assize Courts were rebuilt in 1826.

Of the medieval fortress, the walls and gates contain much still of interest, and although much has been lost, valuable records were made of many details last century by the castle surveyor,

E.J. Willson. The wall was up to 6 m thick, and 9 to 12 m high. There were two mottes, the original or 'Lucy's Tower', surmounted by stone walls added in the late twelfth century though now surviving to only half their original height. It lies in the south-western corner. At the south-eastern corner is a mid-twelfth-century tower, crowned with an 'observatory' tower by the prison governor John Merryweather in the 1820s, ostensibly to watch for attempted breakouts but really so that he could indulge his passion for observing the stars. At the north-eastern corner lies Cobb Hall, containing remains of a gaol in its basement. It was used for thirty-eight hangings between 1814 and 1868, often with crowds numbering thousands to watch the spectacle.

The East Gate, the main entrance from Castle Hill, belongs mainly to the thirteenth century, having been damaged in the battle of 1217. In its heyday it was an impressive structure, but its external barbican towers no longer survive above the modern ground level. The West Gate, in contrast, only reopened in 1993, is largely of twelfth-century date. Here the barbican has also disappeared and the external tower to the north was a later, thirteenth-century addition. Observations of works connected with the construction in 1992–3 of the new entrance bridge noted a wall running westwards across the ditch, probably to support a causeway rather than the more normal timber bridge. Immediately north of the Norman gate was its Roman equivalent, again a single carriageway topped by a tower. It was exposed inadvertently in 1836, when the landlord of the adjacent Strugglers Inn was attempting to extend his garden by removing the base of the bank. Fortunately it was depicted by two different artists before it started to collapse and had to be reburied in the bank. There it still lies.

In the outer bailey there were several churches, including that of St-Paul-in-the-Bail, whose cemetery may have extended at one time as far south as Gordon Road, the parish boundary. But, while medieval houses abound along its streets, few discoveries have been made about the medieval city from other excavations in the Bail.

The Cathedral and Close

William rewarded another Norman supporter, Remigius, from the abbey of Fecamp, with the bishopric in 1067. At that time the see was still at Dorchester on Thames, the diocese being the largest in England. The new king's policy was to base his sees in major centres, and Lincoln was chosen for the site of the transfer in

Seal-matrix of walrus ivory, possibly that belonging to Hubert, papal subdeacon, in Lincoln 1072–3: found during excavations at Hungate in 1985

1072–3. Remarkably, the writ giving the new bishop the right to move the cathedral still survives as part of the dean and chapter archives, and is now in Lincoln's Cathedral Library. Although little is known about Remigius himself, he appears to have been a competent bishop, and one of the new king's closest allies. He set up a new chapter on a secular model, perhaps because of the need to recruit many new canons. During his episcopate he was faced with a number of problems, including an attempt by the Archbishop of York based on the seventh-century conversion of Lindsey by Paulinus to claim the diocese for its own jurisdiction. This matter was only resolved after Remigius' death in 1092. By that time his cathedral was only days away from consecration. The choice of the Lincoln site, in the south-eastern quarter of the upper Roman city, may have been made with the help of papal legates, and it is to one of these that a seal-matrix of walrus ivory, found in excavations in 1985, may have belonged.

Thus began the creation of Lincoln's greatest monument. The cathedral has countless admirers, not all of them Christians, and many of them the people who live and work in sight of it. Lincolnians are undoubtedly very proud, and justly so. It is regularly featured in books and television programmes about medieval architecture, and in addition to the usual cathedral services, is often used for concerts, some of them broadcast. (Regular attenders of such events know that the acoustics are not the best, and in winter, the cold penetrating: blankets, hot water bottles and hot drinks are essential.) Its architectural beauty, and its scale, enhanced by its hilltop position, have drawn many favourable comments, such as those of the nineteenth-century critic John Ruskin: '. . . the Cathedral at Lincoln is out and out the most precious piece of architecture in the British Isles and, roughly speaking, worthy any two other Cathedrals we have'. The commentator, William Cobbett, writing in 1830, called it simply 'the finest building in the whole world'.

It is not so surprising that it has such an effect on us, for it is a *huge* structure: for two and a half centuries, until its central spire blew down in 1547, it *was* the tallest building in the world, at 180 m (482 ft) high. Even now that tower, spireless, is 82.5 m high, while the cathedral measures almost 150 m long and is over 50 m wide in places. As it now survives, it contains work and styles of several different ages, although its principal elements are Norman (at and behind the west font), Early English Gothic (1192–1300: most of the rest), and some later additions and changes.

The building erected by Remigius was in contemporary Norman style, and is most closely paralleled by St Etienne at Caen. A recent reinterpretation of certain features at the west end by Richard Gem, based on a contemporary reference to a 'strong church with strong towers' has suggested a defensive function may have been partially intended, owing to the insecurity of the times. There are indeed fortress-like features including machicolations for dropping missiles. Others have suggested that some French models also incorporated a number of military-type elements, and that no military purpose would be intended. Here at the west front, some original late eleventh-century niches are still visible but much was lost in the fire of *c.* 1141, which led to a rebuilding in more decorative style being ordered by Bishop Alexander. Contemporary Italian and French influence is clearly discernible in the new west doorways and in the frieze above, one of the cathedral's architectural glories. It shows scenes from the Old and New Testaments. The frieze, much weathered already, is currently being protected from the elements, and a great debate is taking place as to whether it should be removed permanently and housed in a new gallery nearby. Unfortunately the rest of Alexander's church was destroyed when an 'earthquake' split it asunder in 1184. Sceptics have suggested that the real problem was structural: defects in the new stone vault, or simply poor building.

That second tragedy provided the necessity for Lincoln to be rebuilt, into what survives today as the greatest example of Early English Gothic architecture. The origin of the new campaign is associated with one of Lincoln's most revered bishops, Hugh of Avalon (1186–1200). A Carthusian monk from the French Alpine region, he was selected by King Henry II for the Lincoln see. Although by all accounts an austere and saintly person – he was canonized in 1220 – he strongly defended the Jews against persecution, and was able to influence both Henry and his successors, who were much affected by his death: this is clear from the surviving account of his funeral, which had to await the return of his body from London where he had died.

The new building began in 1192, funded partly by contributions from local peasants – the swineherd of Stow, symbolic of this gesture, was immortalized in stone at the north-west pinnacle. The decision was taken to change to the Gothic style, with pointed arches, rib vaults and large windows. The details of the work which took the next century to complete are remarkable, and would require several days' first-hand explanation. Only the choir and the east transepts were complete by the time of Hugh's death in 1200, and

The Angel Choir: a view looking north-eastwards

progress was at times slow. The main transepts and their windows followed, and the Chapter House also belongs largely to the 1220s. The collapse of the central tower in 1237 meant that a replacement had to be designed – it was only finally completed, with its tall spire, early in the next century. Meanwhile the nave had followed by about 1250, and the 'Angel Choir' by 1280. The construction of the choir had involved demolishing more of the Roman fortifications (they had already been breached in *c.* 1200), but the space created allowed for a new shrine for St Hugh, a place of pilgrimage. The consecration ceremony in 1280 was attended by King Edward I and Queen Eleanor as well as several bishops. Mystery plays became commonly performed: they were recently revived. Later work included the cloister (*c.* 1300), towers, the new window in the south transept (the 'Bishop's Eye'), and a new window in the west front. Several chantries date from the fifteenth and sixteenth centuries. The so-called Honywood or Wren Library above the North Cloister was built in 1674 to a design of Sir Christopher Wren.

This long list of structural changes and additions represents only the barest outline. Some details are no longer original. Restoration began in 1761, and the west spires were eventually removed in 1807 after an earlier attempt to dismantle them had to be abandoned because of riotous opposition: a rare but illuminating example of the Lincoln populace moved to direct action! The current campaign of restoration is a critical and expensive one, and it is also providing an opportunity for some archaeological research. The installation of new electricity cabling in 1992 revealed several graves in stone coffins by the Crossing. From the fine quality of their garments, which are still being studied, they were important clerics of the thirteenth century.

The Cathedral Community and Its Houses

The coming of the new, enlarged ecclesiastical community to Lincoln in 1072 had major implications for accommodation. The bishop himself was endowed with a number of estates which helped to make him the wealthiest person in the city, but he had a duty to help his canons find houses for themselves, as well as for himself. Initially he had a mansion to the west of the castle (where he could also lodge), in the suburb of Westgate or Willingthorpe, on the hillside to the south of the area now occupied by The Lawn. Bishop Alexander (who also built Newark, Sleaford and Banbury castles) was provided with a tower of the East Gate, but in 1137 King Stephen granted him some land south of the cathedral. Perhaps building was deferred because of the cathedral fire: the known remains on that site only go back to the time of Bishop Chesney, who was given a more restricted area in 1155–8.

Remains from about this date include the East Hall and a recently discovered south range. As the household increased in size and as architectural and living styles changed, so the palace was modified. A new west range including a larger hall was begun under St Hugh and completed by his successor, Hugh of Wells. The other major phase belonged to the mid-fifteenth century, when Bishop William Alnwick created domestic arrangements for himself in contemporary fashion. The tower by which the palace ruins are now entered is the principal remnant of this campaign. Although it welcomed royal visitors in the seventeenth century, the fabric was already decaying. It was damaged at the time of the Lincolnshire Rising and again during the Civil War, after which it was no longer habitable. Apart from his castles referred to above, the bishop also had several other residences in Lincolnshire at Nettleham, Louth, and Stow Park as well as beyond the county. From c. 1660 his normal residence was at Buckden in Cambridgeshire, but the return to Lincoln began in earnest in 1885. Bishop Edward King had a house rebuilt adjacent to the ruins of the medieval palace, which also underwent restoration. Since 1945, the bishop has lived on the north side of Eastgate, in another of the cathedral properties which have surrounded the minster since the middle ages.

Remigius had created a chapter of twenty-one canons. His successor had doubled that number. Their various residences, modified or rebuilt, lay in Minster Yard and to its east and north: there was a song-school by the mid-twelfth century, and a house for the choristers a century or so later, situated next to what became the house of the chancellor in 1321. Properties were gradually purchased by the canons and some bequeathed, so that by about 1300 enough were available to be allocated by chapter as canons came into residence. Another separate community was gradually being created within the city, with – like the castle – its own judicial rights. It felt vulnerable. There were complaints after the building of the Angel Choir had removed part of the city wall that criminals transgressed nightly and that muggings and burglaries were commonplace: a salutary reminder for today's age!

Following a petition by the then bishop, Oliver Sutton, Edward I granted a licence in 1285 allowing the construction of a wall to protect the cathedral's community and its property, with gates locked overnight. The grant was confirmed thirty years later. The Close Wall, initially to be 12 ft high but later heightened and crenellated, took several decades to complete. Some lanes had to be blocked off.

The Bishop's Palace: looking northwards from the kitchen courtyard between the two halls to the Alnwick Tower

Vicars Court: looking north-north-west

There were impressive gateways, the best surviving example being that of Exchequergate, the inner of a double gate. Pottergate is a late nineteenth-century restoration of the original.

Among the houses it enclosed, many have been the subject of recent detailed surveys, which have related what can be said about their complex architectural development against the historical background known from documents. They represent an attractive and impressive ensemble, too large to describe in any detail. Many people's favourite is the chancery (No. 11 Minster Yard). The chancellor's house had been in Eastgate until 1321 when it was considered too small by the incumbent, Anthony Beck. He obtained permission to exchange it for the present site. Its front range was rebuilt in the late fifteenth century: the earliest surviving brick building in Lincoln. It is also notable because of its association, when a widow of her first husband, with Katherine Swynford, whose life was reconstructed in Anya Seton's eponymous novel. She married the widower John of Gaunt, the Duke of Lancaster, in 1397. In her second widowhood she lived in The Priory, No. 2 Minster Yard. By the fifteenth century, and in contrast to the earlier years when accommodation was scarce, it was proving difficult to find tenants for all the properties, and some were demolished.

xchequergate: looking east

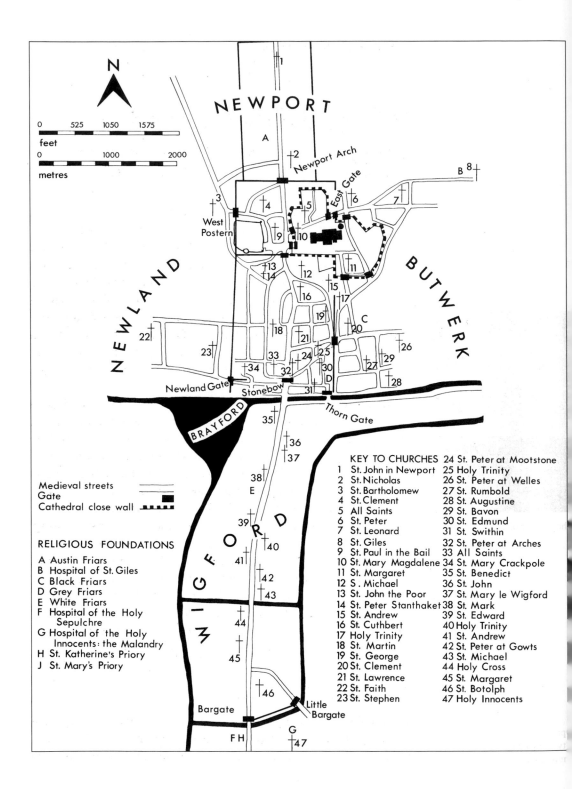

N

| 0 | 525 | 1050 | 1575 |

feet

| 0 | 1000 | 2000 |

metres

NEWPORT

A

Newport Arch

East Gate

B 8

West Postern

3   4   5   6   7

9   10

13
14   12   11

16   15

17

22   18   19   C   20

23   21   26

33   24 25   27 29

34   32   30   28
D
Newland Gate   Stonebow   31

Thorn Gate

NEWLAND

BUTWERK

BRAYFORD

35

36
37

38
E

39
40

41
42

43

44

45

46

Bargate   Little
Bargate

F H   G
47

WIGFORD

Medieval streets
Gate
Cathedral close wall

RELIGIOUS FOUNDATIONS

A Austin Friars
B Hospital of St. Giles
C Black Friars
D Grey Friars
E White Friars
F Hospital of the Holy
     Sepulchre
G Hospital of the Holy
     Innocents: the Malandry
H St. Katherine's Priory
J St. Mary's Priory

KEY TO CHURCHES
1 St. John in Newport
2 St. Nicholas
3 St. Bartholomew
4 St. Clement
5 All Saints
6 St. Peter
7 St. Leonard
8 St. Giles
9 St. Paul in the Bail
10 St. Mary Magdalene
11 St. Margaret
12 S. Michael
13 St. John the Poor
14 St. Peter Stanthaket
15 St. Andrew
16 St. Cuthbert
17 Holy Trinity
18 St. Martin
19 St. George
20 St. Clement
21 St. Lawrence
22 St. Faith
23 St. Stephen

24 St. Peter at Mootstone
25 Holy Trinity
26 St. Peter at Welles
27 St. Rumbold
28 St. Augustine
29 St. Bavon
30 St. Edmund
31 St. Swithin
32 St. Peter at Arches
33 All Saints
34 St. Mary Crackpole
35 St. Benedict
36 St. John
37 St. Mary le Wigford
38 St. Mark
39 St. Edward
40 Holy Trinity
41 St. Andrew
42 St. Peter at Gowts
43 St. Michael
44 Holy Cross
45 St. Margaret
46 St. Botolph
47 Holy Innocents

CHAPTER FOUR

The Medieval City: 1066–1485

The Charter of 1157

T he Close Wall completed in the fourteenth century had expanded the walled area in a new direction. Lincoln grew in other directions too, and defensive systems were built extending the lower Roman walls down to the new riverfront, and to protect the two suburbs of Wigford and Newport. By 1350 then, the growth of medieval Lincoln was complete: more than that, it had begun to shrink and to enter a long but uneven process of decline. The factors which contributed to growth and subsequent decay, and their impact on the city – in particular the physical manifestations – are the subject of this chapter.

For most of the people of Lincoln, the Conquest would have represented no more than a passing background event in their lives, and Scandinavian influence was still felt for several decades. The Norman Conquest had not seen an immediate increase in prosperity. In fact, just the opposite occurred. Relocation of those displaced by the castle and cathedral (some perhaps to the suburb of Newport) and documentary evidence for further devastation point rather to a temporary setback. Nor was the subsequent improvement steady, thanks partly to the effects of royal battles, royal impositions and occasional fires. But it is clear that by 1150 the town was again amongst the most wealthy in England, and for the following century Lincoln seems to have been in the forefront of urban prosperity. Henry II's agreement to a charter in 1157 (it still survives), and his wearing of the crown in his palace in Wigford that Christmas confirmed Lincoln's prominent place on the national scene.

Trade and Privileges

opposite: map of the medieval city showing the many parish churches, c. 1300

Central to the economic basis were the cloth industry and wool trade which operated on an international scale, working through Flemish merchants. Lincoln and Boston both prospered greatly from the trade: in 1202 merchants from the two towns paid more tax between them than London. Wool came from the Midlands down the Trent and Fosse Dyke, thence to France and Flanders. Foreign merchants and other non-Lincolnians involved in the trade had to buy the right to operate through Lincoln. It was obviously worthwhile. Good communications were essential: the clearing out of the Fosse Dyke in 1121 had provided a link to other centres accessible via the Trent, while wool from Lindsey long-wool sheep was of very good quality.

Reconstruction of a medieval loom (built for the *Lincoln Comes of Age* exhibition, 1984)

The weavers of the city were sufficiently established to set up a guild in 1130. They made 'Lincoln' cloth, especially its fine dyed 'scarlet', but also woollen cloth in (off-)white, grey and green. It had a wide reputation, enhanced subsequently by the legend of Robin Hood. (A modern version can now be bought in the city.) When the cloth trade subsequently declined owing to Flemish competition, the failure of local merchants to modernize, and to the introduction of fulling mills, best located by upland streams, Lincoln's economic status was badly affected. The city might still export local wool, but, not being labour-intensive, it did not yield the same as actually manufacturing cloth. The collapse of weaving had an effect on the local economy far beyond the weavers themselves, for many others were dependent on them. Sources of imported pottery found in excavations are a clue to the city's trading contacts: a change in pottery types in the thirteenth century reflects the breakdown of Lincoln's international cloth trade.

Other trades are known partly from personal names in surviving documents, athough they cannot necessarily be taken as definite evidence that the person either still practised the trade or did so on that site. Pottery and tile manufacture normally took place on the urban margins, and three or four kiln sites dating from the thirteenth and fourteenth centuries have been found in Wigford. As might be expected, fishing and related activities were to be found further north in Wigford, in the area of the river. By the end of the fourteenth century, there were eleven trade guilds. Most were under the control by then of the Council: breweries and bakeries could be inspected. The weavers were not subject to such control, nor were they free citizens of the town. A prominent group of merchants founded St Mary's Guild, the premier fraternity, or socio-religious organization, in the city from 1251. It met in Wigford in a fine building which still stands in part, and which may have been designed originally for Henry II's residence at the time of his visit in 1157. Annual feasts and conviviality made up one element of their activities: they also supported each other legally and financially when necessary. There is no exact modern equivalent, but several local organizations operate in similar ways.

St Mary's Guildhall after restoration

The leading merchants of the city were the most prominent element in local government, as they had been before the Conquest. Their economic influence and power gave them that position. During this period, citizens' rights were being gradually established, not usually without some fee being paid to the king, and liberties, some financial, established at Lincoln generally followed the lead of London. One objective was to lease or 'farm' the tolls and taxes due to the king. The charter of 1157 had awarded citizens' rights to new residents of a year's standing who had paid their dues, while a further series of charters began in 1189. In 1194 various new privileges granted included exemption from toll throughout England.

The Council itself contained twenty-four members, half of whom appear to have been of higher status – the aldermen. There were ten officers. Lincoln was early in receiving permission to elect a mayor: the first holder was probably the same man, Adam, who was definitely in post by 1210, and who subsequently sided with the barons against King John. When Magna Carta was drawn up in 1215, one of the official witnesses was Hugh of Wells, Bishop of Lincoln. The cathedral preserved its copy through several centuries. Formerly on show in its library, it has visited North America and Australia on exhibition in recent years. It now forms the centre-piece of a new display in Lincoln Castle.

The Developing Urban Topography

Many of the streets created during the Anglo-Scandinavian period continued in use; others were laid out to link them as the town became more built up. The major change occurred in the area of castle and cathedral, where the earlier pattern was swept away, and replaced by lanes around both the castle ditch and to north and south of the minster. After the choir was extended eastwards, the Close Wall eventually replaced the former city wall as a constraint on movement. Where the new street of Westgate met the Roman west wall a new gate was provided. Further development of the two pre-Conquest suburbs of Wigford and Butwerk (literally 'outside the ditch') took place. They were rich in churches, respectively eleven and six, and both contained some fine houses, Wigford especially: Adam the Mayor was among those who lived here, not far from St Mary's Guildhall. Yet the suburbs would also have contained a high proportion of the poorer elements in society.

It may have been at this time that vertical timber wharves first appeared on the waterfront. Excavations at Waterside in 1988–90 found evidence for extensive reclamation, as a result of which the waterfront was advanced to a point not far from its modern line. Some wealthy merchants' houses were to be built on the riverside nearby. As the population grew and riverborne traffic increased, other areas too were being reclaimed. In between fish traps which were already in operation, waterfront structures have been detected on the north and east sides of Brayford Pool. The area to the north of the Pool was part of the suburb of Newland, known from documents to be in existence by the twelfth century. There was another low-lying suburb at Thorngate, south of the river and east of High Bridge. The bridge itself dates to *c.* 1160: its Norman structure still survives with later additions, including an easterly extension to take a chapel of St Thomas Becket built later that century. Newport (= 'new town') has been mentioned already. It extended for several hundred yards north of the Bail, and had its own market adjacent to one of its only two churches, St John's. These later suburbs are distinguished by the larger size of their parishes.

Newport was certainly provided with a defensive ditch, although nothing has yet been found of its supposed wall and towers which were depicted on some early maps. The ditch appears to predate the fourteenth century. The wall and two Bargates built at the southern limit of Wigford were probably in place by 1217, for repairs were needed to them after the battle of that year. A later date is probable for the extension of the city wall to the river, where it terminated in towers. The western tower, named erroneously as the Lucy Tower, was uncovered in 1972. Its construction in fine ashlar was the final stage of a process of reclamation which went on for over two

Artist's reconstruction of the extension of the city walls to the Brayford Pool. The base of the fourteenth-century tower was found during excavations in 1972 (D.R. Vale)

hundred years after the Conquest. In the early fourteenth century, the king gave permission for houses to be built over the old Roman south wall along the medieval street of Saltergate. Elsewhere, the former Roman walls were reused, and no evidence has yet been found for refurbishment: this might in any case only have been traceable if the wall had survived to its full height. But several new posterns are known.

Newcomers at the Fringes

The mature medieval settlement thus extended in a north–south direction for about 2 miles. At its widest, from Newland to Butwerk, it measured less than half of that. But we have yet to establish how densely packed were the residential properties across much of this area. At the edge of the city were both fields and pastures, lying north of the Foss Dyke and Witham in a wide semicircle. Towards the eastern limit, a little north of the river, a cell of the Benedictine Abbey of St Mary of York was established within half a century of the Conquest. Only a fragment, belonging to a later rebuilding, now survives on the south side of Monks Road; it is cared for by the City Council.

The urban fringe at the southern end of the city had a different history, but here saw several medieval establishments. The Malandry, or Hospital of the Holy Innocents, was the earliest foundation, possibly by 1100. It stood to the south of the later

Bargates east of the High Street. Nearby and across the street was the Hospital of the Holy Sepulchre, founded soon afterwards. Adjacent was St Katherine's Priory, belonging to the only monastic order of English origin, the Gilbertines, whose founder's principal seat was at Sempringham in Kesteven. This dates from the mid-twelfth century and eventually covered a wide area, as well as owning considerable estates. It was active in producing wool. Nothing now stands above ground of these establishments, although building work has yielded architectural fragments from the priory and a coin hoard from the Malandry site.

We have on the whole been similarly unfortunate with the urban friaries which appeared in the thirteenth century. With help from Bishop Grosseteste, the Franciscans arrived in 1231 and were given more land in 1237 in the south-east corner of the walled city. This was as central a site as could be found for a friary – it meant that the City Council had to move to a new guildhall next to the lower south gate, later the Stonebow. The Franciscan buildings extended as far north as Silver Street, near to which remains of the church were excavated in 1973. The 'Greyfriars' further south is probably the first church later converted into the infirmary, and is certainly worth a visit. After the Dissolution it became a grammar school for over three hundred years; for most of this century it has served as the City and County Museum.

Part of the thirteenth-century undercroft of the Greyfriars

The Franciscans had the largest known population of the four friaries, with as many as sixty-three in 1301. The Dominicans, established in 1238, were probably as successful, since they eventually occupied an area of about 10 acres to the east of the lower city and on the hillside adjacent. The Carmelites were based in Wigford by 1269, and had a recorded population in the early fourteenth century of between twenty-two and forty. The southern fringe of their site was partially excavated in 1986 after the closure of St Mark's railway station. The Austin Friars founded their base in Newport before 1280. Each of the religious houses was in competition with the others for resources. It seems already clear that at least three of the friaries were successful enough to be still expanding in the fourteenth century.

Parish churches had continued to grow in number after the Conquest, but not with the same speed as previously. Re-used Roman material was plundered and incorporated into the first stone churches, but is not found later: perhaps the cathedral quarries were made available. From the twelfth century it was not such a simple process to create a new parish: the bishop exercised greater control.

Nor was there the need. The total of perhaps forty-seven churches was more than the medieval town could sustain. Most were always small and could not be maintained by the size of their parish: only fourteen were left after 1549. There was, of course, much rebuilding during the period. In particular, the common cellular-linear Norman plan was often embellished with a west tower and the nave widened in the Early English style. An increase in size was necessary to cope with the growing population, but was also a result of the changing, more elaborate, liturgy: chancels were commonly extended. A similar pattern was found at the two churches which were completely excavated in the 1970s: St-Paul-in-the-Bail, and St Mark, in Wigford. Unlike Norwich, Lincoln's medieval churches have not on the whole survived. The best and most distinctive examples of the Romanesque period are the towers of two churches in Wigford: St Mary, and St Peter at Gowts, while a similar structure is that of All Saints, Bracebridge, a mile or so to the south of Bargate.

Good masons were also in demand as stone houses became more common. A fire like that of 1123 which had devastated part of the city was one good reason for the conversion from timber into stone. But the change might also be seen as a reflection of the increasing wealth of the urban community. Stone became normal from the early thirteenth century, to judge from excavations in the Flaxengate area – which contained some Jewish merchants – and other sites in the town. Floors might be of clay or mortar, and roofs were constructed of tiles. Pits for rubbish were normally to be found in the back yard, while some houses incorporated early 'toilets' in the form of garderobe chutes and pits. Yet the first stone houses, of the mid-twelfth century, may have been exceptional, and confined to those with both the resources and the need to keep them secure. Accordingly the earliest medieval stone residence in the city is also the most famous twelfth-century house in England, the Jew's House at the bottom of Steep Hill. It was certainly occupied by a Jewish merchant from the time of its construction in 1150–60, and may have displayed the arcaded front of a shop. A similar arrangement has been proposed for Lincoln's other Norman House, close to the top of the hill, which probably belongs to the last two decades of the century. It was formerly and erroneously known as Aaron's House, after the most famous moneylender of his day in England, but may actually have been occupied by Joceus of York. Aaron is known from documents to have lived further up the 'Steep', in the Bail. When he died in 1185, vast amounts were owed to him from several hundred borrowers, many of them prominent nobles including the

The Jew's House (left) and
Jews Court

King of Scotland and the Archbishop of Canterbury. A special
department of the Exchequer was set up to deal with the debts!

The Jewish community served as bankers of the day, playing a
significant part in facilitating investment. At this time, Christians were
not allowed to engage in usury, and there was always an undercurrent
of resentment, exacerbated by the freer status which the Jewish
community appeared to enjoy. The Jews enjoyed the protection of
Henry II, but soon after his death in 1189 Richard I's planned
engagements with the 'infidels' in the Crusades provided a pretext for
attacks on them. They sought refuge in the castle, and also obtained
support from Bishop Hugh. Some of those responsible for the attacks
were subsequently punished by fines. The Jews suffered again in the
mid-thirteenth century, not helped by Bishop Grosseteste's more hostile
attitude, and in 1255 Lincoln was the scene of an alleged ritual murder
of a young boy ('Little St Hugh'), the sort of story which was trumped
up against the Jews in several countries. Some Jews were, however,
punished and executed in London. By this time, the Lincoln Jews,
reduced in influence, were sharing a cemetery in York with the
community there. Although a famous wedding is recorded in 1275 at
the building now called Jews Court, immediately to the north of the
Jew's House, in 1290 after further persecution the Jews were expelled
from England until readmitted by Oliver Cromwell. Their absence had
economic implications.

Most of the Jewish community appear to have lived on or near to the main High Street, then called Mikelgate. As such they were close to Lincoln's various markets, which, from being in churchyards, later occupied open areas mainly along that street. The fish market lay at the junction next to the Norman House near the top of Steep Hill, the poultry market on the hill below, the cornmarket just above the Jew's House. The skin and cloth markets were on the next streets to the west. Fish and meat were also available on High Bridge. Fairs were also held, and as today they could be the scene of criminal activity and riotous behaviour.

This picture of the medieval community and its townscape is based largely on documentary and architectural evidence, supplemented by discoveries of identifiable and dated structures in excavations. Archaeology helps to bring home the insalubrious conditions of the medieval urban lifestyle. Excavations have also produced a mass of artefactual and environmental material, good groups of which can be studied to throw light on other aspects of life. For instance, detailed examination of thousands of animal bone fragments from the Flaxengate site provides good evidence for diet and animal husbandry, as well as the organization of the meat supply and on the actual species themselves. During the Middle Ages, cattle, sheep and pig bones dominate the assemblages. All appeared to be fairly healthy animals. There were notable changes in both butchery techniques and in terms of the reduced age of slaughter of sheep and pigs in the third quarter of the eleventh century, perhaps

Excavations of medieval houses in progress at the Flaxengate site, with the medieval street at the right-hand (eastern) boundary

as a response to the dietary requirements of the new Norman overlords. Sheep were no longer kept merely for wool, but were killed earlier for their meat. In time, sheep became more numerous in relation to cattle, and this presumably reflected a change in the economy. An estimation of medieval Lincoln's annual meat consumption puts it in the region of 100,000 kg, a figure which would have required between four and seven hundred of each of the three major species. This has interesting implications for the amount of grazing land which the urban settlement required in order to feed itself.

It is hoped to compare the above results with others from various sites in the city and search for comparisons and contrasts. Similarly, research is also under way to compare pottery – there seems to have been a change in ceramic style, for instance, about 1100 – and other artefacts, so that different social groups might be identified. In this way, archaeology can make a substantial contribution to our understanding of the social and economic life of the city.

AD 1300–1500: a Change for the Worse

Most histories of Lincoln in the fourteenth century begin understandably with an account of Edward I's Parliament, held in Lincoln in January 1301. The king had been in Lincoln since before Christmas, a temporary sojourn on his way north to fight the Scots. While he was in residence, he received and granted a petition from the city for a new charter restoring liberties which had been forfeited in 1290 owing to the unscrupulous practices against their fellow citizens by some of the merchants. The city was also granted the right to levy taxes for six years to repair roads.

This single passage contains a number of themes which occur regularly over the next two centuries or so: visits by monarchs often in need of funds to pay for wars, being exploited by the Council to obtain concessions. Initially these concessions were mainly concerned with civic privileges, later with relief from the burdens of taxation and office. Gradually, but increasingly from the middle of the fourteenth century, the economy of the city was suffering, formerly affluent inhabitants becoming more desperate, and the fabric of the town in decay.

Yet the decline was not an even process, nor did it affect all classes to the same extent. While there were famines in England in the early fourteenth century, the next few decades were more settled. On the whole the lot of the rural peasant was certainly no worse in

1400 than it had been a century earlier, and urban prosperity was based to some extent on that of the surrounding countryside. Town populations were in decline, but population size was not necessarily a reflection of prosperity, and some authorities argue that this could mean more space and a more salubrious environment for those still left. There was certainly a general fall in population in this period.

Whatever the national picture, it is clear that Lincoln did undergo a long-term serious decline from which recovery only began at the end of the seventeenth century. The principal causes were economic, with the loss of major foreign markets for the cloth trade, the relocation of weaving to areas further west, the failure to maintain the Foss Dyke, and competition from Boston and Hull as ports. The city was also marginalized in terms of land transport by the building of the Great North Road. The Black Death of 1349, however serious its impact, was by no means the most important factor. While some building did take place, the general impression is of abandonment and demolition of properties – especially those away from the principal routeways. Public buildings and churches became dilapidated, and repairs, even if achieved, could take many years. Funds which had been granted for repair often went astray as certain classes suffered financial hardship, some wealthy merchants avoided the burdens of office or moved away, and social unrest increased.

Two parliaments took place in the city in 1316, with the war in the north still in progress. The citizens used this occasion to obtain rights to let all of the king's waste land and 'empty places'. A grant of 'murage' in 1322 was a royal indication that maintenance of the city walls was considered vital to protect 'the king's city'. Monarchs could be sympathetic and supportive. They could also place demands on local communities to finance their military campaigns, but here concessions might be offered in return. In 1387 Richard II granted Lincoln's mayor the right to have a sword carried before him: it is still used for ceremonial purposes when the monarch visits, and is on exhibition as part of the Civic Insignia. The sword was often associated with county status, but that was confirmed in 1409 with the granting of the city's right to its own sheriff. Land to the south was subsequently added to the new county, and only in 1974 did the city cease to be a county borough: the loss of status is still resented. The city's first constitution had been effectively laid down in 1422: it set out that there should be a 'commonalty' or general body of the twenty-four existing 'councillors' plus another forty members. The newcomers contained merchants with aspirations to join the twenty-four, and therefore likely to go along with them.

The sword which Richard II presented to the city

Control was still essentially retained by the mayor and his inner circle of twelve, and the poor remained powerless.

By the end of the fourteenth century, the city was petitioning for relief from some of its financial burdens. Among those appealed for successfully, large measures were granted in 1434, indicating that Lincoln was doing badly even by national standards. In 1439, remission was allowed from taxes on export, and in 1446 Henry VI gave tax relief for forty years. Accounts of the state of the city confirm the need for petitions. As early as 1365, Edward III had complained about physical conditions in the city and the effect they were having on trade '. . . such merchants on account of the deep mud and the dung and filth thrown in the streets and lanes, . . . and other loathsome things lying about and heaped up there, come but seldom and thereby the evil name of them and their city grows worse and worse'. The king ordered the city to clean itself up and pave the streets within a year.

It may have been partly due to the effect of civic disorder on the king's attitude, and to subsequent local inaction, that the Staple was removed to Boston in 1369. Lincoln had been one of the Staple towns created in 1326 through which all goods of certain materials, including wool and hides, had to pass. The Staple itself stood on the riverside, a few hundred yards east of High Bridge. The failure to maintain the Fosse Dyke, obstructed frequently from 1335 in spite of funds agreed for the purpose, also reduced Lincoln's ability to function as an export centre. For perhaps two centuries the two Lincolnshire towns had flourished as twin ports. Now Boston gained and for a time eclipsed Lincoln: in 1334 it rated fourth nationally to Lincoln's sixth place. But its fall was to be more dramatic even than that of its local rival.

An indication of the decline in the cloth industry is provided by a document of 1348 in which the city's weavers were seeking relief. Few of them now survived, as against a number of about two hundred in Henry II's reign. In the late spring of the next year, the damage wrought to the general population by the Black Death was devastating. About 60 per cent of the clergy of the city perished, while there were thirty times the number of wills – reflecting the wealthier inhabitants who probably suffered less – than normal. Other epidemics were to follow in the next decades and also occurred in 1457. No wonder, then, that the population was shrinking and with that came physical decay. Although some rebuilding is known from the friary sites and at certain churches, others were in desperate straits. Only fourteen parishes survived after 1549. Two of these, the excavated sites of St Paul and St Mark, actually saw enlargement of the church in the later middle ages but suffered later. A survey of 1428, however, provides a more accurate impression of the city as a whole. Four parishes had no inhabitants – three of these were in Wigford – while seventeen others contained no more than ten persons. Twelve parishes went during the fifteenth century. Being a royal priority, the completion of the town walls (if they were ever completed) was considered vital but was a longer drawn out affair than it should have been in spite of murage grants. The guildhall by the south gate was in such serious disrepair by 1390 that it had to be demolished. Its successor, the present Stonebow and Guildhall, was not finished for over a century. It housed the city prison. The castle too was considered to be of no military value by 1327. Some rebuilding of private dwellings took place, but things were getting worse.

With this increase in poverty came more social conflict, a symptom often found in larger towns when certain elements of society appear to be immune to endemic deprivation. In response to imposition of Poll Tax, raised to cover the cost of the Hundred Years' War, there was a Peasants' Revolt across much of England in 1381. (History does teach us some lessons.) Although no evidence survives that Lincoln joined the rising, some of the blame for the cost of the war was directed at the Duke of Lancaster, John of Gaunt, who was also the castle constable. The house of his mistress and, later, wife, Katherine Swynford, was attacked in 1384, and so were market stalls in the Bail. Ironically, the dispute had to be settled by John himself. He reiterated the legal and commercial independence of both Bail and Close.

Lincoln ended the Middle Ages in a sorry state. Henry VII annulled the acts of Richard III, one of which had provided the city with more 'county' lands. The once confident regional capital was reduced to the status of a county town. From being one of the handful of leading centres from the tenth century, tax yields suggest that by 1500 it was hardly in the top twenty. There was to be no substantial improvement for some time.

A rare sign of late medieval prosperity: an imported lustreware bowl from Valencia in Spain, found at St Mary's Guildhall: early fifteenth century

CHAPTER FIVE

The Lean Years Continue: 1485–1714

T
he economic history of Lincoln in the Tudor and Stuart periods followed the same distressing trend as in the previous century. There is an impression of a more isolated town in a more isolated county, not helped by the constant risk of flooding in the lower part of town and in the lands to south and west. With the continuing economic problems, the physical decay of the city became even more acute, while any increase in population from the mean low of about two thousand was modest and due principally to immigration by the rural poor rather than to an upturn in the city's fortunes.

Lincoln was not alone among former larger centres in suffering this way. York, for instance, underwent a difficult period, though mainly confined to between *c.* 1450 and *c.* 1560. The smaller market towns fared comparatively better. The sixteenth century also witnessed a rise in food prices which affected most of the population, and several plague years in the second half cancelled out any promise of revival for some time.

We have a clearer picture of the City Council's involvement in all this since the surviving Minute Books begin in 1511. They reveal some, at times, violent disagreements. Power seems to have remained with the mayor's inner circle. The Council now met in the Guildhall above the Stonebow (and still does for full meetings). It must have been a desperate period for the Council and regular attempts were made to improve the economy, but with only limited success. It even resorted to appealing for assistance to powerful patrons, among them Cardinal Wolsey, who had been successively dean and bishop in 1509–15 before moving on to York and eventually becoming Lord Chancellor. Henry VIII himself visited in 1541, an occasion for which the city made efforts to tidy up its appearance and made offerings to the royal guest, as well as successfully petitioning him for some remission of its burdens.

The Stonebow, eventually completed in the early sixteenth century

The Reformation and Union of Parishes

The king stayed at the Bishop's Palace which had suffered damage a few years previously because of the unpopularity of Bishop Longland with those rebelling at Henry's radical proposals to break with the Church of Rome. The Lincolnshire Rising of 1536 saw thousands of rebels gather in the Wolds where various Royal Commissioners were present in early October and subsequently move to Lincoln on the sixth. Harvests had been poor in previous years (but not that one) and the imposition of some new taxes caused further resentment. The king sent a letter to encourage the rebels to give up their fight and to hand over their leaders: it contains a phrase describing the county as 'one of the most brute and beastly' shires in the kingdom which has caused considerable amusement since. Several leaders were subsequently executed and certain gentry who were suspected of tacit support suffered the same fate.

For the city, the Reformation principally involved the dissolution of the monastic establishments, a process which began in 1538. It has been described as the greatest act of nationalization without compensation. Apart from the sites themselves, the monasteries and friaries owned large amounts of property in the town. The city attempted to take over St Katherine's Priory and the Monks Abbey: the former became part of the property of the Grantham family, who built a house in the grounds. The Austin and Dominican friaries meanwhile were sold to agents in monastic lands, who had much to dispose of, and their ruins accordingly survived for much longer. The city did have some success. It took over the Greyfriars water supply with its conduit, and built a new conduit outside the church of St Mary Le Wigford to serve that part of town. This still stands, and a recent study of its fabric has suggested that it was formed of re-used stone from the Chantry of Ranulph Kyme, a former bailiff, in the Carmelite friary. Other effects of the Reformation included the removal of cathedral treasures, among them saintly relics. Shortly afterwards, the City Council took over the now moribund St Mary's Guild and its sister organization St Anne's Guild, which had held an annual pageant. In the process, it appropriated the guilds' assets and sold them off before the king had a chance to do so: a case of the disappearing family silver?

The next decade saw a rationalization of the city's parishes, with a corresponding reduction in clerics. Several churches could then be demolished. Incomes were consequently combined, and the 1549 Act achieved its aim in re-establishing some order. Pressure was

St Mary's Conduit, partly built from fragments of an earlier chapel

43

exercised on the community to attend church, especially for the sermons. There were now nine churches left in the city, excluding five others in the Bail, Close, Newport and Eastgate: in his account of Lincoln not many years previously John Leland had referred to a document referring to a former total of thirty-eight (an underestimate, as we have seen in the previous chapter). He also noted the fact that many houses were derelict and in a state of collapse: excavations confirm this state of affairs. Some of the fabric from the churches and friaries was purchased to repair or rebuild houses, as well as for road metalling and the river-wall, and some was used for making lime. The new porch at St Mark's, visible on John Speed's map of 1610 and excavated in 1976, was probably reconstructed from part of a nearby church or friary: there are a few possible candidates. In the same year as the parishes shrank in number, both the diocese and the cathedral's lands were also reduced in area. As if in a symbolic anticipatory gesture, the central spire had yielded to a storm in 1547.

Economy, Society and Culture under the Tudors

The citizens were acutely aware that the Foss Dyke had been a key to former prosperity, and intermittent but energetic efforts were made to improve its state. A commission set up in 1518 had to abandon its task three years later, and attempts were made to persuade merchants in Hull and York to invest in a scheme, while those owning adjacent land were told to weed the dyke and maintain the banks.

Although it remained a political, legal and ecclesiastical centre, the city no longer had its former manufacturing base, but rather, according to one account, lived off its markets and fairs. Victualling, and industries producing leather and metal goods for agriculture were prominent, but attempts to recreate the cloth centre of old ended in failure. More realistic was the petition to Parliament in 1588 to buy and sell wool, taking advantage of an increase in pastoral agriculture. With prices rising, controls were put on traders; the term 'company' now replaces that of 'guild'. Local, approved companies had a monopoly, but regulations were imposed setting out the length of apprenticeships. This all took place against an atmosphere of social problems, necessitating controls on inns to reduce drunkenness and its effects, and measures to deal with the

The Cardinal's Hat, Upper
High Street

poor. An element of charity becomes discernible: parishes had to find work for those in their care. But beggars had to wear badges, and those from outside were liable to be expelled.

In the meantime, there is evidence that the general position of the gentry was improving, and, apart from ex-mayors, candidates were now normally selected from this class to represent the city in parliament. They were less likely to claim their expenses from the Corporation. One of the most distinguished Members of the period was Dr Thomas Wilson, MP 1571–81, who became a Privy Councillor. Some new large houses are known, principally on the main street and in the Close, and inventories from the late sixteenth century give clues as to wealth and lifestyle. Half-timbered buildings of some scale and attraction can still be seen, on Castle Hill (now the Tourist Information Centre), in the Strait and High Street (the Cardinal's Hat, named after Wolsey), and by the river, even on the river: the High Bridge carries a building which, though much restored, is Britain's earliest surviving shop on a bridge. There was more space available if it could be afforded: documents refer

High Bridge: the bridge dates
originally from *c*. 1160, the
building on it from 1601

45

constantly to orchards, gardens, or 'waste', and the suburbs contained some farms. Recent excavation has revealed that the castle's west gate, closed already for some time, now housed a bronze foundry, making, among other things, church bells.

The cathedral was still the main source of cultural development. One of the occupants of Minster Yard for a while was Thomas Byrd, the leading English musician of the Elizabethan era. The school itself was merged in 1583 with the local grammar school, which choristers were helped to attend after their voices broke. Greyfriars was its new base. The Bluecoat school, for twelve boys, was established by the Christ's Hospital foundation under the will of Dr Thomas Smith of 1602. It found its first home in about 1611 in part of St Mary's Guildhall (recent survey identified markings on the wall of a writing test), before moving in 1623 to a new site on Christ's Hospital Terrace near to the top of Steep Hill.

Century of Turmoil

If the Tudor period had been a time of almost unrelenting economic depression for Lincoln, the following century was just as bad in those terms until signs appeared of improvement in the last decade. But religious and political troubles loomed larger than in previous or subsequent periods, as monarchs of different inclinations came and went. James I was in fact quite taken with the city and the opportunities it provided for sport on a week's visit in 1617. The new Stuart king had attempted to weed out Puritan elements, and this policy was later enforced strongly by Archbishop Laud. In John Williams, Bishop of Lincoln from 1621, Laud found an opponent. Eventually the Bishop was committed on a trumped up charge, and sent to the Tower in 1637. The Archbishop was also critical of the state and indiscipline of the cathedral and the city generally. There was some truth in this: the county's clergy was on the whole well educated but not particularly godly. King Charles I had other local opponents in the form of parliamentarians who spoke out against his excessive demands to cover the cost of England's involvement in the Thirty Years' War from 1624. Eventually Parliament was dissolved in 1629. Things had come to a head and the public mood was not helped by the effects of bad harvests in that and the following year, and plague and rioting compounded famine.

Beset by its own internal wrangles (they still happen from time to time) as members gathered around prospective leaders, the City Council also struggled to deal with immigration from the countryside and the control of trading. A new charter obtained in 1628 was little different from the earlier one, but less democratic, eventually helping the gentry class to take a more prominent role after the Restoration. The gentry was also keen to secure the honour of magistracies, in which they administered the Poor Law (established in 1597 and 1601), as well as acting as royal agents in law, administration, and keeping the peace. But leading merchant families continued to exert considerable influence. The mayor in 1642, John Becke, was a son and grandson of former sheriffs and mayors, who were drapers. His son became sheriff, his grandson sheriff and mayor, his great-grandson sheriff and mayor, and his great-great-grandson sheriff and mayor.

In the preamble to the 1628 charter, the city had described itself warmly as 'one of the chiefest seats of our whole Kingdom', and as a major centre of trading activity. In reality its commercial importance could now only be measured in local terms, while the events of the civil wars were to inflict more damage on the fabric and in turn on trade. In those war years of 1642–51 Lincoln's vulnerability stemmed from its location on the 'frontier' between the opposing sides, and military control of the city went to and fro several times during the campaigns. (The dilemma of John Becke symbolizes this position, for although he initially was prevailed upon by the Parliamentarians not to publish a royal proclamation, he later changed his mind under pressure from Charles.) The king was said to be well received by large crowds on his visit to the city in July 1642 – and certainly the uphill clergy and gentry were behind him – but opposition forces were in control soon after his departure.

Thus began a period of five years in which the city changed hands several times. It fell to the Royalists in May 1643, soon after Cromwell himself had been in Lincoln. Parliament took it back in October after the Battle of Winceby. By the following March Prince Rupert's soldiers were in command, but only for several weeks, as the Earl of Manchester retook the castle for the king's opponents and made the city his base. He used as headquarters the Angel Inn, which used to stand at the corner of Bailgate and Eastgate. The upper town was subsequently pillaged by the conquering troops. Much greater damage was inflicted during the second war, when a small Parliamentary force based in the Bishop's Palace was stormed by Royalists. They were in turn shortly to be defeated in battle at Willoughby in Nottinghamshire.

Many of Lincoln's surviving medieval buildings had been badly damaged. The episcopal palace, which had undergone some restoration under Bishop Williams, was set fire to and became so ruinous that it ceased to be used as a dwelling. The great hall provided an excellent site for a rabbit warren. The palace was sold off, together with some of the houses affected. As well as these, two uphill churches had been destroyed, others burnt or severely damaged. The cathedral itself had been subjected to further ravages – especially to its windows, brasses and monuments – and restoration took several decades. The Close's administration was in 1657 passed (temporarily) to the City Council. The castle's gaol and courts were now in need of repair. Some of the rubbish cleared from the streets was dumped in garderobes in Vicar's Court and in the former Roman well next to St-Paul-in-the-Bail.

Lincoln had paid a heavy price, and yet there was sufficient disenchantment with Parliamentarian rule for the city – like the country as a whole – to welcome the Restoration and to return two Royalists as Members of Parliament in 1660–2. There then followed an official purge of puritans from the local administration, and Nonconformists were less tolerated, as the squires and the Church of England reasserted their authority. The cathedral chapter had all to be reappointed after the war with the exception of the Archdeacon. One of the new appointments, Dean Honywood, commissioned the new Wren Library as well as overseeing the fabric repairs.

The city treated the new monarch with circumspection. That did not prevent its being perceived by Charles II along with other towns as centres of opposition, although Lincoln was clearly not in this category. The king ordered that the town charters should be surrendered in 1684, and Lincoln's was handed over to the infamous Judge Jeffreys. Its replacement issued in the following year was if anything more restrictive, but its reception still occasioned some festivity: the 'conduits ran claret'. While Charles II was an astute and generally popular king, his brother, James II, who succeeded him, alienated the country by his blatant Catholicism, which led to his replacement by the new Protestant monarchs, William and Mary, in 1688. James' demise gave a pretext for an attack on the Jesuit school. Nonconformists, on the other hand – Quakers, Baptists, and Presbyterians – were grudgingly tolerated. The Quaker Meeting House, one of the earliest survivals in the country, was built in 1689 on land purchased for burial purposes twenty years earlier. All went smoothly when King William visited the city in 1695, and handed back the sword of Richard II offered to him by the mayor. One outcome was the granting of a new September fair.

Artist's reconstruction of the
Friends' Meeting House, built
1689 (D.R. Vale)

Economic Gloom: a Silver Lining At Last?

James I had helped organize a collection for the Foss Dyke in 1617
but it remained ineffective as a commercial route for another sixty
years. An increasing demand from the end of the century for the
county's wool from the West Riding cloth towns made the dyke's
clearance even more urgent. In summer, it was almost dry. The Foss
Dyke was still in a bad state in 1672, the year after a new Act was
passing for its reopening: but work now began, and cargoes passing
through Lincoln steadily increased in scale. But attempts to re-
establish the city as a key element in the wool trade led again to
failure. Lincoln's bad economic condition was dependent on its
location and the prosperity of its rural hinterland. Plagues occurred
several times between 1610 and 1631, and more efforts had to be
made to deal with the effects of poverty and hunger, as price rises
continued.

The city had no major industry, no significant outlet to the sea and
it was badly placed in relationship to the two great towns in the east

of the country, London and York. In the latter half of the seventeenth century the country became more prosperous, its agricultural productivity improved, profits accumulated from the new colonies and the explosive growth of London stimulated the nation's economy. Lincoln was not well placed to take advantage of any of these trends; the benefits of its fertile southern regions and its wool either went straight to London or bypassed the city by the great routeways of the Trent, the Great North Road and the sea.

The late seventeenth century saw the dire state of the city commented on by various travellers: some of these have been quoted in the Introduction (p. vii). Lincoln was essentially now a one-street town, though this was, admittedly, a long street which contained some fine houses. Most markets were still held on the High Street; and the new fair from 1695 noted above was for horses, beasts and goods. The Corporation was still having difficulty in controlling outside traders. Some local tradesmen had resorted to producing their own tokens from 1656 when the coinage supply was disrupted for several years. Many have survived. There was a city halfpenny in 1669, but the practice was forbidden in 1674. Another common practice, that of selling civic freedom, was also banned in 1685.

An insight into several aspects of social and economic life of the late seventeenth century is provided by the survival of nearly six hundred probate inventories, lists of goods which had belonged to newly deceased persons. These corroborate other evidence indicating that gradually the city was coming to share in the greater national wellbeing. The uphill residents were the wealthiest on average in the city and the best houses lay in the Close. The most densely populated parishes, in contrast, were downhill. The inventories also provide some clues to the occupations of the people: eighty-one different occupations occur but there are some obvious omissions, and others are underrepresented – ale brewing (a profitable activity at the time), civic officials, and labourers, for instance. Among the unusual jobs, Lincoln had one of the earliest toymakers in the country. Lists of house contents are enlightening in themselves, and allow us to contrast the material culture of the wealthier tradesmen and gentry with that of the poor. Predominant among prized possessions of all classes was an impressive bed! To judge from the distribution of landownership and personal contacts recorded in the inventories, Lincoln was beginning to exert an economic influence much wider than that of a market town. It extended over much of the county, for which it also served as an administrative and social centre. It was acquiring the attributes of a modest 'provincial' capital.

An imported 'Delftware' tile of the late seventeenth to early eighteenth centuries, found in excavations east of Brayford Pool. It was probably made in Holland or Belgium

Wages were rising, plague was a thing of the past, and new building was to be seen. The upper city was witnessing the first signs of revival, with the construction of a new shire house and prison, and work on parish churches. The social life of the gentry was focused above hill. A new house of correction appeared and major roads were repaired and cleared. The grammar school was flourishing, and some boys went on to Cambridge University; clergymen's widows devoted many hours to teaching poor children. Houses were being modernized. The latest buildings, like the Friends' Meeting House, were now built of brick. By the end of the century the population was definitely on the increase, but still well below that of the Middle Ages. A recent estimate suggests about three thousand five hundred in 1661, about four thousand five hundred by 1714. Although various factors militated against any hope it might have of regaining the status of a regional capital such as Norwich or York, the eighteenth century was to be the start of a new era for the city.

CHAPTER SIX

Revival and Growth: 1714–1837

T
he Georgian period witnessed a marked change in Lincoln's economic fortunes, in the lifestyle of its inhabitants and in its physical condition. Improvement began, slowly, in the last two decades of the seventeenth century, and accelerated throughout the eighteenth. The major factors were the Agricultural Revolution, which was making its mark by 1750, and the stimulus to the local economy from improved communications. The period saw the great eras of coach and canal travel; the Industrial Revolution arrived in Lincoln only with the coming of the railways. As time went on, an increasing proportion of the growing population found work in the town, but there was also much poverty, and, arising from it, crime and challenges to established authority.

The contrast between growing industry downhill and the affluent citizens of uphill was strong. There was another life for the wealthy, with a greater variety of goods and social activities on which profits could be spent. Moreover, the gentry continued and developed its enthusiasm for recreations, such as horse races and balls, while the 'Age of Enlightenment' produced a series of antiquaries. Throughout all these changing circumstances, the social and civic calendars with their established rituals provided a framework of continuity which helped the community retain some links with its past traditions.

At first, Lincoln remained a mere county town, whose hinterland was rich in agricultural production, but difficult of access to the outside world. It may have been isolated, but the city's ancient remains were visited and described by a growing number of antiquaries, among them William Stukeley. They were just in time: some Roman and medieval walls and monuments had survived in a remarkable state to this period, but much was to be lost as building activity accelerated over the next century. A great deal must have been re-used in new structures, although Stukeley's map of 1722 shows some quarry pits to the east of

Part of Samuel and Nathaniel Buck's *South-west prospect of the City of Lincoln*, 1743

the upper city. Thomas Sympson, who wrote a tract on Roman Lincoln, complained that a single ex-mayor was the only councillor he could get to take an interest in or aid his researches. (It *has* been a struggle at times.) One of the county's leading figures, Sir Joseph Banks, was initially a botanist who accompanied Captain Cook on his voyages while a young man, and was later President of the Royal Society. He later caught the antiquarian bug, and helped open the shrine of Little St Hugh in the cathedral. He is reported to have found the remains contained in a kind of pickle, which he tasted! He lived to recount the story. E.J. Willson, the county surveyor in the first half of the nineteenth century, recorded a great deal of the city and county's ancient monuments, many of them now lost, and his books are a valuable source of reference for modern research.

The change for the better was not at first apparent. Daniel Defoe visited Lincoln first in 1712 as a government official. His description of the lower city, published in 1724–6, as '. . . ragged, decayed, and still decaying' hints at almost terminal decline. Fragments from formerly grand ecclesiastical edifices had been used to construct even pigsties. Yet he did find the upper city congenial

for its architecture and for the company it provided, while noting that the best area for trade and business was the steepest part of the hill. Loveday, writing in 1732, recorded that brick had been used for some of the better new buildings, but many were 'mud-and-stud' and still had thatched roofs. D'Isney Place on Eastgate was a fine town house of that decade: it survives as an hotel. Among other contemporary residences are the Number Houses immediately west of the cathedral, so-called because they are thought to be the first in the city to be graced with numbers. Much of the fabric elsewhere in the city remained 'ragged' for several decades. Only two churches had services every Sunday. One of them, St Peter at Arches, was rebuilt in 1724 by the council. St Mark's and St-Paul-in-the-Bail were only rescued from collapse sixty years later.

The Number Houses in Minster Yard, seen from the west front of the cathedral

Communications

The Act for the new turnpike was passed in 1756, making the Close the main thoroughfare through the city. Road traffic was increasing,

stage-coach services were introduced (though they did not become regular before 1784), and inns were needed to revive weary travellers. The construction in 1786 of the 'New Road', now Lindum Road, made the approach to the upper city less demanding – though it still defeats some vehicles. But the reopening of the Foss Dyke was a greater stimulus. The Council lived to regret its agreement of 1740 to lease the dyke for 999 years to Richard Ellison for a modest annual payment. Works were completed by his son four years later: he made himself a personal fortune as profits from tolls increased severalfold, and understandably the Council was forever damned. Ellison was also a partner in Smith's Bank, established in 1775–6 with his agent Joseph Brown, an ex-mayor, and with Abel Smith of Nottingham. Credit was now available for expansion, and it was made use of: the bank's turnover was soon of huge proportions.

Coal was one commodity whose price was immediately reduced by the improved state of the Foss Dyke, but much went in the opposite direction too. During Georgian times Lincolnshire's main contribution to the Industrial Revolution was to supply food to the teeming populations of London, the industrial midlands, and Yorkshire. Wool was still important at first, but in spite of local efforts was losing out to cotton; corn was sent to West Yorkshire. The county's potatoes found a new market in Manchester after canal links were completed. The Witham was also improved, and the Brayford was to develop into a busy port, surrounded by warehouses and boat-yards. The increase in river traffic and works on the river to provide new wharves required a vast new army of workers. Many

lived in St Swithin's parish along the north side of the Witham, one
of the poorest parts of town. Here were located too most of the
makers of clay pipes – an occupation of low status. For the first half
of the eighteenth century, tobacco was popular with all classes; later
the gentry rejected it in favour of the more fashionable snuff, but the
numbers of pipe fragments found in later archaeological levels
indicate that the ordinary people stayed with tobacco.

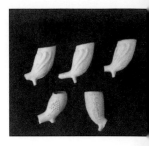

Some decorated clay pipes of
the mid-nineteenth century,
found in recent excavations

Much of the responsibility for order in the town lay with the
parish officials, among them the constable and the churchwarden.
They were also expected to administer poor relief and to repair the
local streets, and to collect rates to pay for municipal enterprises.
The Corporation itself helped with the principal highways and
managed charities. Control of trading was no longer practicable:
tailors and shoemakers were the sole surviving companies. The city
was represented in parliament by those who could afford the
substantial costs of elections.

Increased Productivity

During the later part of the century radical changes were introduced
into agriculture, which allowed farmers to obtain greater yields. The
two essential components were enclosure and drainage. Roughly
contemporary was the Industrial Revolution, in which Lincoln was to
play a major role later, particularly in producing machinery and goods
for agriculture. Much larger vessels, up to fifty tons, could reach the
Brayford Pool by 1820, and twelve years later the Steam Packet
Company began regular operation to Boston. After pressure from the
city, a new bridge across the Trent was constructed at Dunham in 1834:
and to the frustration of travellers at busy periods, it still exacts a token
toll. There was a surge in economic activity and in the population,
punctuated only by the insecurity and costs of the war with France
which ended with Waterloo in 1815. By 1801, the city contained over
seven thousand inhabitants – for the first time for five hundred years.
Numbers were rising by about 15 per cent (i.e. well over a thousand) a
year, mainly by natural growth, while houses actually doubled in
number in the first thirty years of the nineteenth century. Although for
most, standards were improving, the number of poor also increased,
and their living conditions worsened. Many of the new houses were
badly built tenements. For the first quarter of the nineteenth century,
the parish of St-Paul-in-the-Bail had the highest ratio of illegitimacy in
England: it contained a house for pregnant spinsters! So much for the
affluence of the upper city. There were other problems connected with

increasing urbanization and industrialization. Water quality suffered: it was the start of the modern era of industrial pollution.

Expanding Social Horizons

The cathedral clergy were among the leaders of society, but often absent from the city at their other residences. James Yorke, dean in the 1760s and '70s, later took up the bishopric of St David's in Wales but managed to retain the Lincoln post at the same time. This was a period when the cathedral was undergoing repairs, but also had to reconcile itself to losing the west tower spires in 1807. The letters of his wife, Mary Yorke, to her friends furnish an interesting perspective on the city from one who had travelled and seen much. Like many used to a more cosmopolitan environment, she had problems adjusting to the provincial atmosphere of the county town. While her visitors might enjoy the busy social rounds of balls, plays, dinners and teas, she found the quiet times tedious, and noted that the local people's main concerns seemed to be with eating, attending church, and playing cards.

For the gentry, however, this was on the whole a good period. The regular round of the Assizes coincided with increased recreational activity. Horse racing, which had begun in 1597 on the heath to the south of the city, later transferred to a new course on the Carholme. The grandstand (now a listed building) was erected in 1806. The Lincolnshire Handicap was first run in 1849: it continues as the first 'Classic' in the year on the 'flat', but was transferred to Doncaster when Lincoln ceased to be part of the first-class circuit. Several balls were held each year, including some in race week. Initially they took place at the steadily decaying Angel Inn, but in 1744 new Assembly Rooms were built on Bailgate: the delightful interior still survives, but the rooms now play a quieter role in community life. Downhill society was given its own assembly in 1787 over the Butter Market, built in 1736 north of the Stonebow out of the profits of civic banquets. The market façade was subsequently dismantled and re-erected to serve as a market hall south of the river. A small theatre existed from 1732, near to the castle, hence the name given to adjacent 'Drury Lane'. It moved to its present site behind Clasketgate in 1736, and was rebuilt in 1806. Walks and parks were created, for fairweather, fashionable strolls. That in Besom Park, over the line of the old Roman west wall on the hillside, belongs to the 1720s. Its line is now followed partly by the street known as 'The Park' and Motherby Hill to the north. Temple Gardens, a park near the later Usher Gallery, was created by c. 1815.

Artist's impression of the hillside from south of the Stonebow, *c.* 1790. St Peter at Arches and St Martin are visible, the latter beneath the County Hospital of 1777 (D.R.Vale)

We see also the beginnings of public services. Although the Lighting and Paving Act was not passed until 1828, in the meantime, much developed to help mind and body. The County Hospital moved to its second home near to the top of Steep Hill in 1777. It is a salubrious, south-facing site: the location favoured for town villas 1,500 years previously by the Roman well-to-do. The building is now occupied by the Lincoln College of Theology. A new asylum – The Lawn – was established nearby on Union Road in 1820 under the reforming spirits of Drs Willis and Charlesworth, who believed in not restraining patients. This too had extensive grounds, as its name implies, and liberating views southwards. On its closure in 1985, it was purchased by the City Council and is now a successful visitor and conference centre, including a display about the history of the hospital and its place in the treatment of psychiatric patients. Edward Charlesworth's statue stands at the corner of the grounds. It was also on his initiative that the first Lincoln library began, operating by subscription. Reading rooms had been provided for newspapers earlier in the century. The first permanent newspaper, the *Lincoln, Rutland and Stamford Mercury*, opened in the city in 1784.

Educational opportunities were still limited, but the Christ's Hospital School was expanding both physically and in terms of its curriculum, which was becoming slowly more liberal. A Sunday school for the poor was established in 1785. Other poor were kept busy at the House of Industry west of the castle; it was full by 1789, but only yielded to a larger Union Workhouse in 1837. Charitable

The neo-classical frontage of The Lawn hospital, restored to its former glory

...lis' Mill on the Lincoln ...dge, the only survivor of a ...w of several windmills

bodies grew. National Schools began to appear early in the nineteenth century. Friendly Societies are also known. The Mechanics' Institute of 1834, based in the Greyfriars, symbolized the start of adult education, and other societies were formed for those with the resources and time to follow their interests. There were also places of harsher lessons. A new Sessions House and city prison at the bottom of Lindum Road succeeded the gaol in the Stonebow, whose atrocious conditions had been criticized. A new county gaol was built in the castle in 1787 and enlarged in the 1840s. Nearby Shire Hall, built in 1776, suffered subsidence and had to be replaced in 1826 by the present building.

Some fought strongly against crime and drunkenness: the Temperance Movement arrived. Nonconformist chapels sprang up in several parts of town, and of increasing size. There were eight by 1826. The small Unitarian chapel of 1725 still survives on lower High Street, but the later Wesleyan and other chapels were built to accommodate over a thousand worshippers.

Such was the city on the eve of the Victorian era and even faster industrial growth, events which coincided with fundamental political changes. The Reform Act of 1832 and the Municipal Corporations Act of 1835 made significant alterations to the structure of the Council and its electorate. The Council was now to contain twenty-five members, including representatives covering Bail and Close. Civic expenditure was cut back, and the plate was sold off. Councillors would be elected for a three-year term. The new electorate voted in a new, reforming group of candidates at the next elections. Society was becoming more complex, and more democratic.

CHAPTER SEVEN

Industry and Expansion: 1837–1914

T he Victorian era witnessed the greatest period of the city's growth, an expansion closely related to the successful development of an engineering industry. Notable among Lincoln's manufacturing firms were companies who competed successfully in the international market for agricultural machinery. Their ability to trade was facilitated by the coming of the railways which could transport coal and iron efficiently. The growth of the Victorian period was more than a continuation of trends begun in the previous century: the sheer size of the city and nature of the new employment brought social changes and problems, but also the resources to provide public amenities and services. By 1911 a population of over sixty thousand was made up of a more complex, stratified and regulated society than ever before, with its distinctive 'urban consciousness'. It ceased to be a purely county market town, and power was being democratized. New building of every type – civic, commercial, ecclesiastical and residential – was necessary; much of it has now disappeared, but only in recent decades has its architectural style found general appreciation.

Railways: the Catalyst

To those accustomed to the convenience of main-line railway travel, Lincoln can seem a bit of a backwater. It might not have been thus. Owing to the suitability of the flat Witham Valley, the city could claim the distinction of having been the subject of the largest number of projected railway schemes anywhere – over eighty – but only a few ever came to fruition. The greatest disappointment, then as now, was that the main Great Northern Line by-passed Lincoln, running instead, like the Great North Road, through Newark and Retford and closer to the major population centres of

Nottinghamshire and South Yorkshire. The route adopted was only one scheme out of several, but it was the single scheme which avoided Lincoln! That the city lost out was partly due to the enthusiasm of the Member of Parliament for Doncaster, which itself might have been by-passed if a Lincoln route had been adopted. Lincoln's cause was not helped by the chaos which reigned at a public meeting held in the castle to discuss the project. Nevertheless a Great Northern loop line came a few years later, and eventually trains travelled out of the town's two stations in seven directions.

Because of the rivalry between two companies, with the two stations came two crossings on the High Street. This situation lasted until 1985. Amid large crowds and with great celebrations the first line to arrive was the Midland from Nottingham in 1846. It operated from St Mark's station, now closed (the structure may soon be restored). The Great Northern loop followed in 1848, and was supplemented in due course by the Manchester, Sheffield, and Lincolnshire Railway (supposedly known to investors as 'money, sunk and lost'; to passengers as 'mucky, slow and late': trains have always been easy targets). The railways had a major impact on their competitors; coaches and road transport could not compete until mechanization and mass production arrived. Waterways were used less, their cargoes being now confined largely to heavy goods such as grain. There was also a major physical effect on the town; the tracks and sidings occupied a huge area, and the rail companies became property owners on a large scale.

Artist's impression of the Great Northern level crossing, late nineteenth century (D.R. Vale)

Heavy Engineering

Local engineering companies actually turned out some locomotives and coaches, and a few later products, such as Ruston and Hornsby shunters, have survived. But their principal *raison d'être* was to manufacture machinery which made agriculture more efficient; ironically, so that more urban industrial workers could be fed enough to produce other machines! The firm of Clayton and Shuttleworth was the first in the city to rise to prominence. From its base at Stamp End (on the river east of the city), it made steam engines, threshing machines, and, by 1845, portable engines which were exported widely in Eastern Europe. Within twenty years it had well over a thousand employees; in forty, more than twice that number, and many based abroad. Other companies included that of William Foster (later to be associated with the tank) and Robert Robey.

The city bedecked for the visit of King Edward VII to the Royal Show in 1907. There was industrial unrest at the time and severe unemployment the following year

Axonometric view of the
Maltings (Dawber's?), built
within St Mary's Guildhall

Robey's introduced some new products: winding engines for
collieries, and electric lighting power for the City of London. It
won a gold medal at the Paris Exhibition in 1878 for its
achievements, a feat emulated in 1900 by Ruston & Proctor. In
1856 the young Joseph Ruston became a partner in the firm of
Ruston, Proctor & Co., and travelled widely to market its
products. By 1890, there were over one thousand six hundred
employees and Ruston was a wealthy man. He had dabbled in
public munificence and liberal politics, and built up an impressive
art collection at his mansion at Monks Manor. Over half a century,
then, expertise had been accumulated in engineering skills which
had gained an international reputation for quality. The firms
survived in something approaching their original form into recent
years, gradually being merged into larger conglomerates.

There was a range of other industries across the city, some of them
occasioned by its expansion. Brick and tile for new building was a
case in point: at one time the six brickyards could not cope with the
demand. Some served agriculture: the prominent windmills along the
edge north of the city were replaced by steam driven versions, and
factories producing fertilizers were built. Others supplied social and
cultural needs: breweries known included that at St Mary's
Guildhall, of which remains survived to be found in 1982. It was
probably developed on a larger scale, about 1880, by the local firm
of Dawbers. Former maltings still stand adjacent to the Brayford
Pool. Boats and organs were also made in this vicinity, and bicycles
elsewhere in the town. Workers had to be housed, many close to
their workplace, but some had to be transported: a horse-drawn tram
began operation to Bracebridge in 1883. It was replaced in 1906 by
an electric version which initially employed an unusual stud system
for power transference, before conversion to the more orthodox
wires.

A larger population also needed more clothing and foodstuffs and
the retail trade developed considerably. They included the Co-
operative Stores, first established on its present site on Silver Street
in 1861 before expanding into many branches; department stores
(often family firms with a paternalistic approach to their employees),
and Boots the Chemist. By 1860, Sincil Street housed a row of
shopkeepers between the river and the railway station, adjacent to
the market: the cornmarket was moved nearby in 1846 – the streets
were no longer adequate – and rebuilt on its present scale in 1880.
Both street and building have survived to function successfully in a
new age of retail.

Population Growth and its Results

One of the earliest photographs of the city: High Street near to the Cornhill, *c.* 1873

While the middle classes found new opportunities for enhancing the style of their fashions and their residences, for the majority of workers life was much harder. Many moved into the city from outside: natural growth could not produce the rapid increase in population, as Britain underwent the world's first great urbanization. Although Lincoln was not in the fastest growing category, figures available from the census make the rate of increase clear. At the beginning of the century, Lincoln had again reached its medieval high of about seven thousand, and this figure was more than doubled by 1850. By the turn of the next century, the population was almost up to fifty thousand, and still growing quickly. New housing areas were found across the river from and linked by a new bridge to Clayton and Shuttleworth's factory. Two hundred houses were built in the period 1851–5. Many of Robey's workers were housed west of Canwick Road, close to the factory, and other areas north and south of the historic core were infilled with terraces. The areas along Burton Road and in the West End followed at the end of the century. Many of these new units, especially the earlier constructions, were barely adequate in terms of space, and poor living conditions were exacerbated by the pollution caused by industry, the general filthy conditions in the town, and an insanitary water supply taken from a polluted river. The dispensary was busy issuing cures, and the hospital was moved to its present site between Greetwell Road and the hillside in 1878, but political action was required to attack the causes rather than the symptoms.

Political Change

Electoral reforms had a major impact on the city's political stance, especially in the immediate afterglow of new elections. Ceremony was dispensed with for a while. Reactionary Conservatives such as the eccentric Colonel Waldo Sibthorp, MP, who died in 1855, became anachronisms. Already his family had abandoned their mansion near St Mark's church for Canwick village. Among other legendary actions, Sibthorp had argued successfully, against the wishes of both party leaders, for a reduction in Prince Albert's grant. It was later suggested that this was the reason that Queen Victoria, on a later visit by rail through the city, never left her carriage! The second Reform Bill of 1867 brought the working class into the electorate. In this new atmosphere Joseph Ruston was one of those returned as a Liberal candidate for the city until Lincoln was reduced to only one parliamentary seat in 1885. There had been a strike at Ruston's for better wages: his response had been to claim that he needed good profits to pay for his 'bread and cheese'. It was to be next century before there was a successful Labour Party candidate.

The City Council avoided for as long as possible the political unpopularity of levying a rate, and was slow in implementing the Public Health Act of 1858 which gave powers in respect of highway repairs, planning and waste disposal. Private companies for a number of services had existed for some years – the Lincoln Gas Company as early as 1828 – and the benefits they brought were plain to see. Street lighting reduced the incidence of night time crime. Responsibility for sewerage was pressed on the city by the government in 1876, and eventually a $2\frac{1}{2}d$ rate was introduced which allowed the Council to set up and control a number of essential services including gas, water, electricity and the library. In 1906–7 a new service was provided in the form of a museum in the old Greyfriars building.

Lack of water purity remained the principal hazard, but it took a devastating typhoid epidemic in 1904–5, which claimed about one hundred and thirty lives, before serious action was taken. A new supply was found at Elkesley in Nottinghamshire, whence water was pumped across the Trent and to a tower in Westgate which was completed in 1911. It still stands, one of the city's tallest monuments: there are welcome proposals for it to be cleaned and partly opened to public view from 1994. The City Council's position was strengthened with further reforms in 1888 and 1894, whereby it became a county borough, a status which it held until 1974. But by the turn of the century, civic responsibilities were onerous and central government support was necessary.

Services were at last improving. Poverty was a more constant feature. Some of the poor and destitute could find a basic diet in the strict regime of the Union Workhouse, which was rebuilt on a larger scale in 1839. Its numbers had to be increased as it now served a wider area and poverty was more apparent in those early years of the industrial period. Later in the century, living and working conditions began to improve. A major force for progress was the Lincoln Trades and Labour Council, established in 1892, which campaigned for an eight-hour day. Wages were not generally increased until they were standardized after 1918: in the meantime, many local workers had to put up with wage levels more common in agricultural employment.

Education and Recreation

At least their children were soon able to hope for a better future, thanks to the expansion of education. Many new schools opened in the second half of the century, most under the auspices of the Churches. They included a School of Art and Science, later supplemented by technical subjects to form the City School, based on Monks Road. Its façade of 1885 has since been incorporated into a recent addition to the current College of Art and Design. The grammar school moved to a new site on Wragby Road in 1907, where it later merged with the Christ Hospital School for Girls, founded on Lindum Road in 1892 to a design of the local architect, William Watkins: this building also forms part of the same college of art. The curriculum for younger pupils had been widened by 1856 to include the three 'r's'. There was also a diocesan training college (now Bishop Grosseteste College), on Newport, and a college of theology, which took over the former County Hospital site on

Façade of the College of Art
and Science on Monks Road,
built 1885, and later the City
School; now part of the
College of Art again

Wordsworth Street. The chancellor, its nominal head, provided
evening classes for adults at the Central School in Silver Street.
Illiteracy was less prevalent by 1900.

Library facilities were also expanded. The Co-operative Society
had provided a library and newsroom for its members well before
the first public library was created in a room over the Butter Market
in 1894. In 1913 it was transferred to the present building in Free
School Lane, built with the aid of a Carnegie grant and designed by
Sir Reginald Blomfield: he was also responsible for the Usher
Gallery fourteen years later. The leading local newspaper, the *Echo*,
is celebrating its centenary in 1993. It moved to offices in St
Benedict's Square in 1897: these lasted until new technology was
required in 1984.

By the end of the nineteenth century, opportunities for recreation
had grown to include the races, theatre and music hall, football
(Lincoln City was established at Sincil Bank in 1884) and cricket
matches, trips by the train to the seaside, and parks. Temple Gardens
on Lindum Road was emulated in 1872 by the grand opening of the
Arboretum, twelve acres of ornamental gardens on the hillside north
of Monks Road close to the County Hospital. Vast crowds were
attracted by a procession, bands playing, a balloon ascent and a
fireworks display. The new park had a moralistic purpose: to
encourage families to relax together and especially to keep father
away from the public house and other temptations. Band concerts
were held regularly – they were revived recently – and groups came
from neighbouring towns to admire the scene.

Physical Growth

The city's spread to north, east, west and south meant that the simple uphill–downhill contrast of old in wealth and culture was no longer so real, although it was still felt in many quarters. Urbanization brought in its train suburbanization: many of the more affluent members of society went to live in the suburbs. The great industrial magnates had huge town residences built, but the old country gentry no longer figured in civic politics and tended to operate solely from their rural bases. At the edge of the city were market gardens supplying the local population. Beyond were villages from which many now commute to work in Lincoln: that process began a century ago. There were some continuities apart from civic ritual, church services, and the cathedral bells. Inside the ring of industrial housing lay the central business and commercial centre, including shops, banks, the riverside and the railways. The Cattle Market was given a new, more convenient, location on Monks Road in 1849. High Street traders were none too happy at the loss of trade this involved, but consoled by the recent

Saltergate, looking west, in 1901 before it was widened

Two Corn Exchanges still stand in the city centre, but the buildings are now used for retail and leisure

arrival of the cornmarket. There were also horse and sheep fairs. That much survived of Lincoln's former market functions.

The new structures of the period were principally of brick, with slate roofs. Some incorporated cast iron girders. There were new barracks on Burton Road for the Lincolnshire Regiment in 1878. Among the earliest rebuildings of the late nineteenth century were several churches, begun at St Nicholas in Newport to a design by George Gilbert Scott, later of St Pancras fame. Bishop Kaye (1827–55) had rationalized clerical livings and created the impetus for replacing the inadequate 'mean little buildings' by the newer, larger places of worship demanded by the growing populations. St Swithin's church, finished in 1870, was the first of a clutch of new edifices. It was closely followed by St Mark's and St-Paul-in-the-Bail (both have been since demolished and their sites investigated). The cathedral's central tower required serious attention. A new Roman Catholic Church of St Hugh arose in 1893, and several larger Nonconformist chapels were also created: in 1851, at least half of those who worshipped were non-Church of England (Wesleyans were particularly numerous), while up to a half of Anglicans did not attend. Religious belief may have been on the decline late in the century, although it had held up in the more uncertain earlier decades of industrialization. A new period of uncertainty was to begin for the whole country as local volunteers gathered by the grandstand on West Common before embarking for France and conditions they would gladly have swapped for the grime of the factory.

CHAPTER EIGHT

The Twentieth Century

Water-Carriers and Camels

The Great War took away nearly a thousand of Lincoln's young men; a memorial was raised in 1921 by St Benedict's church, and it still serves as a focus for remembrance services. Although not strictly comparable, the city's contribution to the war effort in machine production was at least as substantial, for it provided the first tanks and built many airplanes.

The firm of William Foster had been established over half a century earlier, as a flour mill. Like others in the city it had later specialized in agricultural machinery. At the outbreak of war, some of its tractors were employed to haul heavy artillery. It had tested tractors with caterpillar tracks: this principle was seen by the War Cabinet (Winston Churchill was First Lord of the Admiralty) to provide a means of crossing the intractable ground of the combat zone in northern France. Lloyd George described it as 'an engineers' war'. In an atmosphere of the utmost secrecy, Foster's managing director, William Tritton, was asked in 1915 to produce, with the greatest urgency, an armoured version suitable for the atrocious conditions. The project was code named 'Water-carriers for Mesopotamia', hence the more popular 'tank'. In just over a month, the prototype was being tested in the presence of army experts near to Foster's factory south-west of the city (now near Tritton Road). Its inadequacies were corrected in the next design, known as 'Big Willie' or later 'Mother', and full-scale production began early in 1916. By September, it was in action, and received an excellent tribute from the British commander-in-chief, Earl Haig. The British Army was thus given a major boost in morale as well as an important fighting force. Foster's pressed on with continually improving designs, and produced several other versions of the tank

One of the Lincoln-built tanks, decorated with the 'oriental eye' indicating that it was a sponsored present from Burma to Britain for the war effort

before 1918. Tritton was later knighted. In 1984 Ruston apprentices restored 'Flirt', a mark IV version; it is on display at the Museum of Lincolnshire Life.

A roughly contemporary development during the war years was the involvement of Ruston Proctor and other local companies in the production of military aircraft. Again speed was essential and the whole process from contract to delivery in 1915 took only six months. By 1918, over a thousand planes, each sporting a winged imp, had issued from a growing factory, and in all nearly three thousand, plus many spares, were produced. Together with the products of Clayton and Shuttleworth and Robeys, Lincoln made more aeroplanes during the war than any other city in Britain. The

Ruston's 1,000th aeroplane, completed January 1918

most common was the Ruston Sopwith Camel. It fought, and landed, with distinction – on 3 September 1916 the first enemy aircraft brought down 'on British soil' – a Zeppelin – was the victim of a 'Camel' attack in Hertfordshire. When two collided over France, their pilots landed both safely.

Industrial Change and the Second World War

These achievements were so much the greater in that none of the firms had any previous experience of aeronautical engineering. Yet Ruston's factory had grown to employ about three thousand, many of them women. Foster's too, and other local firms, were busy during the war, but with its end they shared in the slump. Some other towns in the region fared better than Lincoln. Making use of their newly gained expertise, however, Ruston's (now Ruston and Hornsby) diversified into producing cars until 1924. Although they planned to compete with economical models from abroad, their sturdy, solid manufacture and the resulting high price denied the cars success in terms of sales volume and production was halted. Some firms now collapsed completely, or were merged with others: Clayton and Shuttleworth, in dire straits, saw a liquidator appointed in 1930. Parts of the operation were sold to other firms or survived as independent companies. One such was Clayton-Dewandre, which occupied the huge 'Titanic'

Aerial view of the city centre, 18 November 1917. Note the factories (lower right), and terraced housing on the hillside

factory east of the city, so called because it was built in the same year and to the same length as the ill-fated cruise-liner. Yet there was some new employment in the inter-war years. The Smiths crisp factory in Bracebridge created many new jobs in 1938.

More production was of course necessary in 1939–45, and engines, tanks, and tractors, as well as munitions, were turned out in great number. The city's central location in an area of abundant RAF bases meant that many of those who shopped and socialized in the city, and travelled in their thousands via its railway stations, were soon flying over Germany, some never to return. The Dambusters raids, which flew out from RAF Scampton, north of Lincoln, saw public celebration of their fiftieth anniversary in May 1993. Although the city itself was not so seriously affected by bomb damage as some other towns, there were many incidents of casualties and structural damage, several in the Monks Road and Lower High Street areas, as well as on the urban fringes. A Luftwaffe aerial photograph which survived clearly identifies and marks out the major production centres as projected targets.

Contemporary view of the lower part of the city centre looking east, showing the Brayford Pool and railway to its south; industrial works at the top

Although some traces of the engineering firms remain, even the name Ruston has been lost in recent years: it now forms part of European Gas Turbines. Policy for these ever greater companies is normally controlled from outside Lincoln, sometimes from outside Britain. The city has had to diversify, and other forms of engineering, including semi-conductors and electronics, are now on the scene. New companies are being attracted by the relatively low cost of land and by the quality of life.

Expansion at the Fringes

Population growth in this century has been at a slower rate than in the previous two, even falling slightly during the rapid expansion of surrounding dormitory villages, as people sought more space and a generally higher living standard. Many of the city's worst Victorian slums were cleared, and large new estates developed by a City Council keen to ensure adequate housing quality. These included inter-war developments at St Giles on the north-eastern fringe, and Boultham to the south-west, which incorporated a

The north-east part of the city, showing the residential growth at the fringe; top left is the Ermine Estate East, top right St Giles' estate with the recent Nettleham Fields and Glebe Park developments beyond

park. Of some planning renown is the Swanpool garden suburb, on land actually acquired by Ruston. A huge scheme was projected, whose designers had previously worked on a similar project at Letchworth. In the event, only part was built, comprising 113 houses, but still large enough to exist successfully as a 'village' on the edge of town. It is now a conservation area. Since the war, other extensive estates have grown up at Birchwood and the Ermine, west and north of the city respectively, and most recently several private schemes have raised the population well in excess of eighty thousand, with more planned. At the south-western fringes, along and to the east of the Fosse Way, the township of North Hykeham forms part of the agglomeration, but anomalously belongs to North Kesteven District (based in Sleaford) rather than to Lincoln, at least for the time being.

Movement

The modern city required transportation systems, shopping and educational facilities, and cultural and leisure activities commensurate with its size. Bus services were introduced in 1920 (the trams were given up in 1929), but cannot easily be profitable in a city of Lincoln's size and shape. Many workers travel daily by private car: in spite of the opening of Pelham Bridge in 1958 and the 1985 closure of another level crossing, the journey from the southern

The last tram, 4 March 1929

75

'Trips week' at Lincoln
Central station in the 1930s

end of town can be particularly slow. Thankfully, an inner ring road
proposal which would have split the city centre in two only got as
far as its initial phase, Wigford Way. On the other hand, the western
relief road, opened in 1985, has been a great boon to the city in
environmental terms, as well as offering some new views. It has also
made apparent the need for an eastern counterpart, now at planning
stage. In the city centre, while Broadgate remains busier than the
A1, pedestrianization of the central shopping area has proved a great
success, in spite of the problems it can bring for both the disabled
and servicing and delivery. There are welcome moves to slow down
motorized traffic in the uphill historic core, but these have not yet
found favour with all residents and traders: living and trading in
such an attractive and popular environment have concomitant
irritations and constraints, and that fact must be realized by those
charmed enough to settle there. There seems as yet no easy solution
to the problems of heavy traffic filing east of the cathedral. Nor has
the difficulty of moving easily between the Bailgate/cathedral area
and the High Street ever been overcome, and those who trade on
Steep Hill benefit from the harshness of the ascent. There were
proposals for a funicular railway as long ago as 1909 and its
desirability has been raised frequently: even now, a feasibility study
is due to be undertaken by Alpine specialists.

The Urban Fabric

Neither the inter-war years nor the third quarter of the century were vintage years for architecture in British towns, and the demolition of buildings of those periods will be regretted by few. Concrete, sometimes with a brick face, appeared commonly from the 1950s and '60s in the form of Pelham Bridge, the Co operative Store on Silver Street, Danesgate House on Clasketgate, three high rise blocks of flats and the Eastgate Hotel. Many now wonder how some of these buildings could have been allowed. One scheme was not, although it features in the first edition of Pevsner's *Lincolnshire* as though it would be built: the Sincil Street Civic Centre. Like the early 1970s 'brutalism' of City Hall and the nearby Divisional Police Headquarters, and the offices and car-parks around Brayford Pool, they were simply the style and fashion of an age that believed in 'newness'. At the same time, there are some modern buildings of more lasting merit on the basis of their interior design, such as Damon's restaurant on Doddington Road, St John's church on Ermine East, the Yarborough leisure centre, the maternity wing of the County Hospital, and the new magistrates courts at St Mark's.

The conservation movement has now the upper hand, and is well ensconced. The current laudable policy in Lincoln is that new buildings will only be allowed if they represent an improvement on the existing. Hence, the Waterside Shopping Centre, opened in 1991, even though externally a combination of classical, medieval and Elizabethan pastiche (sometimes termed neo-classical and neo-vernacular), represents by its variety and quality of build a major step forward from the little lamented 1960 extension to Woolworth's or the mass of the adjacent former cinema (the cinema facility itself is another matter). The development of the market area, the successor to the abortive Sincil Street scheme, marked the change in direction; it involved both conservation and new building.

Thanks to the pressure exerted by local historical and architectural associations several historic buildings were saved and restored in mid-century and fortunately the forces of preservation prevailed when the Roman 'Newport Arch' was seriously damaged in 1964. One of the few areas of regret is that the wealth of earlier remains has tended to overshadow those of the industrial period, and losses have included Foster's Britannia Works, where the tank was developed. Conservation policies were initiated in earnest with the designation of the city's first conservation area, covering the historic centre, in 1967. Now Area No. 1, it is officially recognized as being

A view of the top of Steep Hill, showing the Norman House (left), and the Harlequin bookshop (half-timbered building)

of national importance. Other conservation areas have followed, buildings have been listed, and both standing monuments and parts of the city have been scheduled as ancient monuments. The city now has a close working relationship both with local amenity societies including the Lincoln Civic Trust (1954) and the Lincoln Society (1971), and with English Heritage which has brought grants towards various conservation schemes: but these are not achieved without a substantial financial commitment from the local authority. The city has taken on responsibility for a number of historic structures, including standing Roman remains and the Norman houses, and is making sure that these are recorded and interpreted as well as maintained. English Heritage is in the process of a major recording and repair programme at the medieval Bishop's Palace, and is funding the preparation of detailed reports on archaeological discoveries. Even larger programmes of restoration are under way at the castle and cathedral, which are now receiving government help. There are also excellent facilities and extensive expertise in historical and archaeological research, based within the City Archaeology Unit, the County Archaeology Office, the museums, and the Archives office. Local interest is well served by a number of societies. Lincoln has become a model city for historic conservation.

Cultural Life

Several new schools have appeared since the war to cope with the growing need for secondary education. These have remained comprehensive, in spite of some tinkering with their status in the past few years. Further and higher education are expanding, and colleges are developing formal links with universities in the region. The impending arrival of a new independent university community south of Brayford Pool should give both an economic and a cultural impetus to the city centre. It will be welcome, especially since the rationalization of arts associations has meant that Lincoln must now look to Cambridge for grant aid; formerly, the regional body was based in the city. The Theatre Royal, saved by the City Council, is now in private hands, and survives largely on travelling productions with 'star' names. There were at one time eight cinemas. Lincoln now has only one – the Ritz – and that used for concerts on certain nights. Although the Ritz has benefited from considerable investment, further choice is overdue.

The Edwardian interior of the Theatre Royal

Similarly widespread frustrations were felt over the loss of horse-racing since 1964, like the main-line railway over a century earlier, to the rival claims of Doncaster, while Lincoln City Football Club commands a loyal hardcore of support in spite of its ups and downs: at least it is usually higher in the league than Doncaster Rovers these days! Most welcome was the arrival in 1980 of BBC Radio Lincolnshire, appropriately based in the former Radion cinema in Newport. It is very professionally run, and provides an opportunity for all local interests to be given an airing. The independent 'Lincs FM' station has followed. For television, the shape and direction of the hill mean that most Lincolnians take programmes from Leeds, but those south of the cathedral on the hillside obtain a better picture from the Midlands region! Yorkshire Television has its own base in the city, and, as far as I can tell, provides the widest, if not the only, coverage of local events.

With the recent benefit of these communications, many of the citizens are content to live their own quiet lives, belonging to one or more of the myriad social organizations in the area, perhaps to exercise in one of the local sports centres, and to visit the successors of Lincoln's medieval inns, where the quality of food and drink available has risen inexorably in recent years. The Church still plays a major role in social life, of course, many of today's organizations and clubs being Victorian offshoots. The loss of several churches and chapels in the city centre has to some extent undermined this structure, but the redundancies were caused not only by the decline in organized religion but also by the fact that their former congregations had moved away as the parish changed in character from dense terraces to commercial centres and open spaces. St Mark's church only survived so long because of the popularity and magnetism of its final incumbent. When he died in 1969, it was realized that the congregation would eventually drift away to churches in their new neighbourhoods. The loss of these buildings is regretted, but it has been possible to find a new purpose for St Benedict's in the centre as a base for the Mothers' Union, and in 1936 St Peter at Arches was uprooted and its principal architectural elements incorporated into the new St Giles at the heart of that estate.

There is of course no question that Lincoln's people, its council, and its visitors will ensure that the cathedral does not go the same way as many of its medieval churches. It must survive, and it will survive, as a place of worship, a Christian community, and a marvel of architecture. Its links now extend to the diocese of Bruges, a

The cathedral, floodlit, from the west

symbolic commemoration of the commercial relationship with Flemish merchants dating back to the Middle Ages.

There have been civic links with other communities abroad, including Tours in France, but now officially confined to Neustadt an der Weinstrasse in Germany, which was the source of the Christmas Market idea, and Port Lincoln in Australia. Commercial liaisons are being explored further afield. These three themes – the soaring cathedral, the historic nature of civic government, and contacts with the wider world – encapsulate the essence, past, present and future, of 'the place by the pool'.

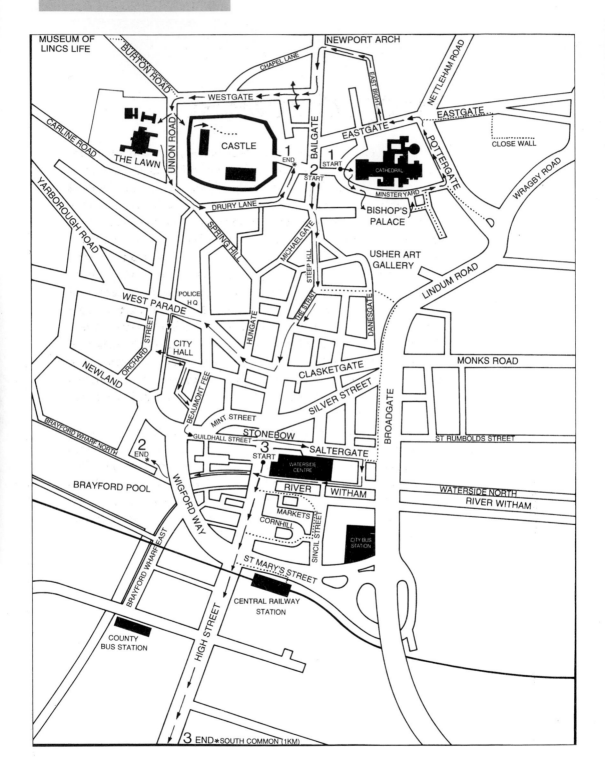

Introduction

Lincoln contains so many worthwhile buildings, sites and attractions that it is difficult to do justice to them all in less than about three days. Even concentrating here on the city centre, as far south as Bargate, the interested sightseer will have to be selective and return to other delights when possible. For the sake of convenience I have organized the tours into three parts, each of which can be enjoyed in about two or three hours by someone walking at a normal pace or by a small group; a large group will probably take longer. They can be easily combined with further elements or a more detailed perusal of the principal historic attractions of the uphill city – the cathedral, the castle and The Lawn, each of which deserves time of its own. These three also form part, together with the medieval Bishop's Palace, of the Lincoln Heritage Trail, on which a free leaflet is available. The trail, which may be extended in the future, commences at The Lawn (where parking, for up to three hours, is inexpensive and spaces are often in good supply).

There are many brief guides and leaflets to aid the walker, some more suitable for educational groups, others for particular themes (e.g. Roman sites) and yet others on particular monuments. The serious student of buildings will be armed with the second (1989) edition of Pevsner's *Lincolnshire*, where fuller details are provided than can be found here or elsewhere. A corrected revision is already in preparation.

Opposite: map of the city showing the routes of the walks

1: The Upper City and the Close

We start our tour, fittingly, by one of the city's most impressive sites, the cathedral's west front.

Some time can be spent here identifying the different architectural elements of the only external face to preserve remains of the eleventh- and twelfth-century work. You can approach the austere original niches and the mid-twelfth-century Great Door, but the frieze is sealed away at present for conservation work: some elements may at times be on display inside the cathedral. Note that the southern half of the front has been recently cleaned: over the next few years other parts of the building will in turn be scaffolded. On the two pinnacles are the statues of St Hugh of Lincoln (to the south) and the Swineherd of Stow (to the north), symbol of the poor peasants who helped pay for the rebuilding begun by St Hugh. The cathedral is open every day but access to some areas is necessarily restricted when services or rehearsals are taking place. No formal entrance charge is demanded but visitors are encouraged to contribute an appropriate amount to its upkeep as they pass the 'pinch-point'. It can be a very cold place in winter. A good impression of the scale of the building can be had from the western end of the nave and also looking up to the vaulting. This view is enhanced if access can be gained to the walkway above the central west door ('Banks' View'). Note the font of marble from Tournai, Belgium.

Make your way up the nave towards the crossing.

As you explore the area beyond the crossing (where tours of the tower begin), it is best to go in a roughly clockwise direction, but keeping an eye on what is visible both sides. I am a particular fan (as are many others) of the blank arcading by St Hugh's Choir, and the

The south transept and the 'Bishop's Eye'

carvings on its screen, but each visitor will be attracted by different elements – perhaps the two great windows in the transepts, the 'crazy' vaulting or the angel carvings of the Angel Choir, the carvings on the screen, the carved wooden bosses on the cloister vaults, the remarkable structure of the Chapter House, the elegance of the Wren Library. The celebrated imp can be found near the eastern end: to its east is the Shrine of St Hugh, now crowned by a modern sculpture. Souvenirs – and they will often include a guidebook – are available in the shop near the west end. There is also a coffee shop, entered via the cloister.

Now go outside via the west door.

Here there is just as much of interest, but details need indicating. Look westwards to Exchequergate, the remaining one of the double gates of the Cathedral Close built *c*. 1320. It was cleaned in 1975 as a contribution to European Architectural Heritage Year. To its right (north) are the Number Houses of Georgian date, so called because they are believed to be the earliest in the city whose addresses were identified by numbers. South of Exchequergate are the former deanery and the old sub-deanery (the dean's house has changed several times; twice in the past twenty years, and it is rather confusing for those not aware of the history of these movements).

Walk eastwards along the south side of the cathedral.

You will come to the Galilee Porch, a processional entrance (now kept closed), opposite which is a door in the wall leading to the medieval Bishop's Palace (English Heritage; entrance charge). The palace is currently undergoing a repair programme which will also see its presentation improved, but information is available on site. The fifteenth-century Alnwick Tower, by the entrance, may include displays on the upper floors about the site's history. Allow half an hour if you want to explore the ruins, which include a twelfth-century undercroft, and the thirteenth-century West Hall and kitchen block to its south. From the southern end of the monument there is a good view southwards overlooking the Lincoln vineyard (planted by vines from Neustadt, the twin city), the grounds of the Usher Gallery, and the eastern part of the modern city across the Witham Gap to South Common.

Return from the Bishop's Palace out on to Minster Yard, or via the arch to the east of the entrance.

Whichever route you take, try to spot the imp that landed on an angel east of the Galilee Porch. Looking south here you see Vicars Court (private). The visible front dates to the end of the fourteenth century and to the right (west) is the fourteenth-century Cantelupe Chantry. A detour down Greestone Place past mainly eighteenth-century buildings will bring you to a postern gate of the Close, recently rebuilt. To the right as you go down the hill is the Tithe Barn with its formidable buttresses, dating to *c.*1440.

Returning northwards to Minster Yard there are more historic houses here on the south and east sides of the minster. Those particularly interested in the Cathedral Close may wish to visit Potter Gate, one of the other entrances: this medieval gatehouse was restored in the 1880s. The chancery is the distinctive brick building: its frontage dates mainly to the late fifteenth century, but incorporates earlier features. To its north is the choristers' house, rebuilt after the Civil War. The most northerly of the range, the Priory (No. 2), now part of the Cathedral School, is well set back from the street. The visible elements are seventeenth century, recently restored, although to its north and east sides are some medieval features including a tower of the Close Wall. A well preserved fragment of the wall defines the northern boundary of the Priory's garden, but the arch spanning Minster Yard opposite, Priory Gate, is a shallow 1816 construction on the site of a former double gate house. On the corner with Eastgate is the building known as the Rest, mainly Victorian in date: it is often open and contains a model of the cathedral when totally 'spired' as well as information on the fabric fund appeal.

The energetic may wish to admire the other attractive houses to the east along Eastgate, before turning right after the Disney Place Hotel, a house of the gentry of 1736, into Winnowsty Lane. Along its southern boundary is another good stretch of the Close Wall, including a corner tower. A further tower is visible from the garden of the hotel. The wall here is due for repair, to be commenced shortly, and not before time: its maintenance is a further burden on the dean and chapter, but with support from the City Council, English Heritage has offered substantial grant aid.

Return to the junction of Eastgate and Minster Yard.

To your left on Eastgate is the statue of Tennyson, a native of Somersby in the Lincolnshire Wolds. More can be learned of the Victorian Poet Laureate in the Usher Gallery, where a special room contains some of his effects. The Central Library incorporates a Tennyson research centre, an important archive used by many scholars (to be housed in Lincoln Castle, 1994–6).

Across Eastgate from the statue is the Eastgate Hotel: at the front of its car-park, the north tower of the Roman gate is exposed after excavation in 1964–6, the southern part of the south tower having been found across the street in 1959. This was a major gate, with a double carriageway. There is a notice-board at the monument explaining the remains, but both this and the walls themselves are currently in need of attention. The curved tower visible is a rebuild of the early third century, replacing a stone fronting of a century earlier which had been applied to the timber structure of the legionary fortress. The medieval gate – which had been built above – formed a temporary residence for the bishop in the twelfth century. A small section of the base of the Roman city wall is visible next to the tower: a longer section of the core may be observed in the hotel's northern car-park.

You may now wish to explore the rest of Eastgate – including first, views of the bishop's house and, next door, the new deanery. The original deanery lay on the south side of the street – the wall west of the Cathedral School buildings retains some of the architectural features. There are more houses of interest in James Street and the north-western part of Minster Yard, by which you can return to the starting point.

For a fuller walk follow East Bight (bight = curving lane), to the left of the Eastgate Hotel.

The much restored Close Wall is on our left for over 200 m, defining the bishop's garden. By the site of the fairly recent redbrick extension to the hotel, a second-century tower and fourth-century thickening were exposed in 1971. But similar features can actually be seen along the north side of East Bight, around the corner, in this peaceful part of the town. Beyond the wall you can get some idea of the scale of the late Roman and medieval ditch: the street beyond, Church Lane, like several more, grew up on the outside of the ditch. A number of houses built in the ditch on inadequate foundations have suffered subsidence: engineers now listen to what archaeologists have to say! As well as the lower courses of the internal tower and the upstanding fragment of fourth-century wall, both repaired with 'sacrificial caps', the line of a Roman water reservoir, or *castellum aquae*, is marked out on the ground. It was excavated in the 1970s and was found to have huge foundations and a solid lining. The overhang on the rear of the Roman wall gives an impression of its height, for it was here before the city wall was thickened. It may have served the Roman aqueduct built to bring water into the city in a sealed pipe from a source to the north-east.

> **Continue westwards along East Bight to the junction with Bailgate.**

On your right is Lincoln's most famous Roman monument, the Newport Arch; the only Roman gate in Britain you can still drive 'through'. But not with a high vehicle, please! It is actually the rear arch of the carriageway of the north gate. It also had side passages; the eastern is partly preserved, while the springing for its western counterpart is still visible: its other side can be viewed from the north together with the front of the semi-circular western tower and part of the later medieval core work. A notice-board has recently been erected to help unravel the confusion. It shows a photograph of the lorry which stuck in the arch in 1964.

Newport Arch, the rear part of the Roman north gate: a view looking northwards

The Roman gate spanned Ermine Street. To the north, along Newport, past the Roman and medieval suburb, it led to a ferry over the Humber and on to York. To the south, down Bailgate, back towards *Londinium*. It is towards London, in this southerly direction, that we now march. Note *en passant* the street of Chapel Lane opposite East Bight. This runs diagonally towards the Roman west gate, and probably originated, like Silver Street in the lower city, as a short cut when the town was fairly deserted and ruinous in the Dark Ages.

As we walk down Bailgate we see the first principal structure, the Methodist church of 1879, followed by a number of charming cottages and larger terraced houses in brick, dating to the late eighteenth and nineteenth centuries. On the left we reach the Assembly Rooms, their Georgian origin now to some extent hidden behind a twentieth-century frontage, but the elegant interior of 1744 still survives in a good state. Access is now easier than formerly:

The incident of 1964 when the arch was almost destroyed: a view looking southwards

during public events (sales, etc.), and when refreshments are available, on an almost daily basis. Opposite, in the cellar of No. 29, are the bases of three Roman columns. These can only be visited in pre-booked groups by arrangement with the private owner. They are the most northerly of a row of nineteen, the frontage of the Roman forum or civic centre which extended southwards for about 84 m (275 ft). The positions of other columns are marked in the street by granite setts – it can be seen from the way Bailgate, the medieval street, deviates from these that the Roman frontage bore little relation to its successor.

Information about the colonnade is available on one of Lincoln Civic Trust's slate panels set on the walls of the Lion and Snake public house. More details and some remains can be viewed as we turn into Westgate and reach the site of the former church of St-Paul-in-the-Bail. Excavations here in the 1970s identified the site of the timber headquarters (*principia*) of the Roman legionary fortress, which was succeeded by the forum of the *colonia*. Some elements of its east range are on view, including a well head structure, while on its courtyard is marked out the plan of the earliest in a long sequence of churches, probably dating back to the fifth to sixth centuries. With the enlightened encouragement of the site's owners, the Parochial Church Council, the remains were laid out in the style of a garden of rest by the City Council in 1983. The plants include a Roman herb garden.

Artist's impression of the
Roman forum and basilica
(D.R. Vale)

The northern boundary of the forum was the north wall of the basilica, or town hall. This still stands to a remarkable height and is known as the Mint Wall. It can be seen from the central part of the St Paul site, but it is worth going up West Bight around the back of the Castle Hotel (originally in 1852 the first purpose-built state school in the city). The wall's base lies over 2 m (about 7 ft) below the modern surface here, giving a total height of at least 8 m. Triple bonding-courses of large tiles were inserted at regular intervals to hold the face and the core together – they have held for over 1800 years – and some of the holes in the wall are 'putlogs' for Roman timber scaffold posts. An interpretative panel is planned by the City Council, which has eventually secured ownership of the monument for 1994.

Returning to Westgate, the tiring walker may wish to continue down Bailgate to end at Castle Hill or to take refreshment nearby.

Alternatively, continue westwards along Westgate past Cobb Hall, at the north-east corner of the castle.

Cobb Hall contained a medieval dungeon and was used last century for public hangings. Beyond is the north wall, the ditch in front now infilled, having been sold off as a way of raising revenue by Charles I. On the north side of Westgate we pass the Old Toy Museum (entrance charge), and another stone edifice by Sir Reginald Blomfield, the water tower of 1911. It was built to house the new water supply from Nottinghamshire after the typhoid epidemic of 1904–5. It may be cleaned and part opened as a public exhibition in the near future.

Immediately beyond is Westgate Junior School, in the grounds of which the Roman legionary fortifications were first discovered in the 1940s: the line of the western defences crossed Westgate, a medieval lane following the outside of the castle ditch, at this point. Opposite is the Strugglers Arms, so named because a gibbet used to stand across from here, at the junction with Burton Road.

You can proceed down Burton Road to visit the extensive collections of the Museum of Lincolnshire Life (entrance charge: season ticket best value), whose popular displays reflect the life of the Lincolnshire agricultural worker of the past two hundred years or so. It also has exhibitions on transport and industry, and on the Lincolnshire Regiment. Beyond, along Long Leys Road and Mill

Lane, is Ellis' Mill (restricted openings; small charge), the last survivor of the row of eighteenth-century windmills on the cliff hereabouts. It has been restored to working life by the Lincoln Civic Trust, and is currently maintained by enthusiastic volunteers.

Back to the corner of Westgate, proceed only a short distance along Union Road past the Victoria public house (the city's best loved 'real ale' hostelry) to the castle west gate.

It sits a short distance to the south of the Roman West Gate, which is buried in the castle bank but was temporarily exposed by the activities of the keeper of the Strugglers Arms in 1836. The castle gate is principally of the early twelfth century. It was only reopened in 1993 after going out of use at the end of the Middle Ages and subsequently being blocked.

You can now choose to enter the castle (entrance charge: again a season ticket to all the County Council's museums represents the best value). It contains much of interest, though in medieval terms it is now merely a shell and its walls have been heavily restored in the last two centuries. There is an almost complete walkway, including the nineteenth-century observatory tower, which provides, via its spiral staircase, panoramic views of the city and country around. An excellent view of the cathedral and the square of Castle Hill can also be obtained

The recently reopened west gate of Lincoln Castle

General view of the interior of the castle, with the former prison building (left) and the Crown Court (centre)

from the east wall. The original keep, the Lucy Tower, has to be visited separately via a flight of steps. At the western end of the grounds are the Assize Courts of 1826. The old prison of 1787 and 1846 lies in the southern part. It now contains a display about the building's history, and more are planned. The Victorian prison chapel, a unique survival, is unmissable for the ruthless skill which went into the design, to ensure that the solitary confinement philosophy of the 'Pentonville system' continued even here. The western rooms of the prison now house an exhibition about Magna Carta, incorporating the Lincoln exemplar formerly in the cathedral. There are other features of interest within the castle; they are described on the leaflet handed out to visitors. They include a gigantic head of George III, which formerly crowned the Dunston pillar, a monument to help travellers find their way between Lincoln and Sleaford. It became a danger to RAF aircraft.

Across Union Road from the west gate of the castle is The Lawn, the former psychiatric hospital built originally in 1820. It was purchased by the City Council after closure in 1985, and has since been converted into a multi-purpose conference and visitor centre, with a number of shops and offices. Entrance to all City Council visitor facilities is, for the moment, free of charge. The grounds cover 8 acres, and a circuit of the buildings is recommended, especially to see the magnificent south frontage with its Ionic columns. Here you can gain entrance to an exhibition about the history of the hospital and its place in mental health care. There is also a restaurant, bar, cafe, picnic tables, and a children's playground. A recent addition is the Dawber Garden, entered through iron gates in the northern wall: it includes some exotic elements based on Lincoln's twin cities. You can also visit a Tourist Information Centre, including a shop which leads to a small aquarium and the Banks Conservatory, named after the Lincolnshire naturalist Sir Joseph Banks. He persuaded the government to send Captain Cook to the South Seas, accompanied him on the voyage, and later became president of the Royal Society. The conservatory contains examples of some of the species he discovered and brought back to England. It is a warm place even in winter, but beware of the sprinklers.

The main building includes facilities for meetings and receptions of various sizes, and from November 1993 will also house the collections of the National Cycle Museum. The separate brick building north of the main block is known as Charlotte House after the first matron: it was formerly the nurses' home, but now provides

Interior of the Lincoln Archaeology Centre at The Lawn

accommodation for the staff of the city's Archaeology Unit. These are private, but the unit and the City Council have created a display on the ground floor explaining a little about the history and archaeology of Lincoln, including some of the processes which are involved. There is an opportunity to handle material and play a number of detection games: it is geared also to the National Curriculum and has been very popular with school groups from the age of seven. An extension is projected.

Leave The Lawn by the main (more southerly) entrance and walk further down Union Road.

At the corner you will pass Hilton House, the residence of the artist William Hilton and regular lodging of his brother-in-law, Peter de Wint, whose watercolours form one of the collections of the Usher Gallery. Opposite is the statue of Edward Parker Charlesworth, the liberally minded physician behind the enlightened regime at The Lawn hospital.

Turn left into Drury Lane (it leads towards the city's earliest theatre), past a row of attractive villas and other houses.

One of them, Castle Villa, shows clear evidence of subsidence from being placed in the ditch fill. There is also a 'folly' of an archway, made up of medieval fragments thought to have come from the Gilbertine priory of St Katherine's, at the southern limit of the medieval city. To the right as we bend northwards is the rear of the Lincoln Theological College, built in 1776 as the County Hospital. The early theatre is now the bistro/bar behind the college and reached from north of No. 1 Drury Lane. Thus we enter Castle Hill, for visitors the principal focus of historic Lincoln.

2: Castle Hill to the River

This walk contains a number of gems which should be included in any general introduction to Lincoln's monuments – the Norman and Tudor buildings and the riverside. It includes much of interest for the eighteenth and nineteenth centuries, but unfortunately shows the worst of the twentieth century. It is all either downhill or on the level.

> **Start in Castle Hill (actually a square, or place), outside the main, east, gate of the castle.**

You can choose to visit Lincoln Castle (two to three hours; entrance charge) from here. The gate itself was rebuilt in the early thirteenth century with outer barbicans, which no longer survive above ground but whose location is marked in the road surface. East of the gate lie the Judges' Lodgings (1810), still used as such, and the building known as Leigh-Pemberton House (formerly offices of the National Westminster Bank) and now the principal Tourist Information Centre.

astle Hill transformed into
market place by the BBC
rops' department for the
lming of *Oliver Twist*,
985

Across Bailgate is the church of St Mary Magdalene, much rebuilt from its medieval state. Although Exchequergate partly conceals the cathedral, the view looking east past all these structures (see front cover picture) conveys a strong sense of history. The atmosphere is sometimes enhanced by street entertainers. The potential of the square for giving an 'olde worlde' feel was fully realized several years ago when it was used as the market place in the filming of the BBC television version of *Oliver Twist*.

Having soaked up the atmosphere, make your way slowly down the narrow cobbled street known appropriately as Steep Hill.

It is an attractive sight, containing a wealth of historic buildings, most now antique or gift shops or offering refreshment to the visitor. There is a recently applied plaque on the wall of No. 33, referring to T.E. Lawrence's favourite haunt when visiting the city (he was stationed at RAF Cranwell), while the appropriately named Wig and Mitre (No. 29) is part of a row of shops dating from the early fourteenth century. Just below here is a stump of limestone on the right-hand (western) side, at the narrowest point of the street. This marks the position of the south gate of the upper Roman city: one of its arches was still partially intact in the late eighteenth century, but the exact plan of the gate is uncertain. There was a medieval gate a little to the south. The last building on the left before Christ's Hospital Terrace is one of the city's famous Norman houses. It dates from *c*. 1180–90 and may have housed some shops from the start.

The open space here is another interesting spot. To the west is the Theological College (formerly the County Hospital) built in 1776, while to the east the College of Art buildings along Christ's Hospital Terrace were erected originally for the Bluecoat School in 1784. Here also was the medieval fish market. The quaint distortions of the Harlequin, now a second-hand bookshop, can also be appreciated a little way down Michaelgate. It is a former inn of the fifteenth to sixteenth century with possibly earlier elements within.

The Roman road here went straight – in flights of monumental steps to cope with the slope. The medieval successors diverge.

Take the route to the left, continuing down Steep Hill past other historic buildings, bookshops and other stores designed partly for the visitor to the city.

One of them, The Pot Shop, on the left-hand side, offers good reproductions of pottery from prehistoric times to post-medieval. The descent offers a good view of the Witham Gap, glacial in origin and a major factor in the choice of Lincoln as the site for a major early centre.

At the bottom of the Steep we find on our right Jews Court, a building of mainly eighteenth-century date and incorporating some elements based on a twelfth-century predecessor, whose site has an interesting history: a well-documented Jewish wedding was held here in 1275. A similar ceremony took place in 1992, the first such for centuries. Jews Court is now the headquarters of the Society for Lincolnshire History and Archaeology, and the society has provided here a well stocked bookshop selling just about every available title (including this one, I hope!) within that wide field.

Next door is the Jew's House, the most famous twelfth-century house in England, dating to between 1150 and 1170. The exterior preserves original features in the form of the door, and first floor windows, and the remarkable detail of the string course carvings. Like its near contemporary higher up Steep Hill, it may have had an arcaded front for shops, but such early use of stone implies both wealth and a need for security.

Opposite is Danes Terrace, adjacent to which remains of more medieval and later houses were excavated in the 1970s. To their south was the Flaxengate site, now a car-park, which produced so much new information about the town in the tenth and eleventh centuries.

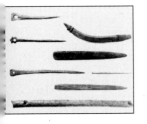

Bone pins, tools and a fragment of a flute: tenth- to eleventh-century finds from the Flaxengate site

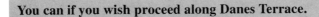

You can if you wish proceed along Danes Terrace.

Here you will find and may wish to visit the Usher Gallery (entrance charge). Its collections include clocks and watches (Usher was a local jeweller who was the great benefactor of the gallery), local topographical studies and watercolours, an extensive collection of early coins, and Tennyson memorabilia. There are also regular special exhibitions. In the grounds you look up towards the Bishop's Old Palace and the cathedral, across extensive grounds first laid out in the early nineteenth century as Temple Gardens, but modified when the gallery was erected. The adjacent main buildings of the College of Art were built as a girls' high school in 1893, and contain a small version of a Greek Temple surviving from the original gardens. The gallery itself was built in 1927 by Sir R. Blomfield in a style reminiscent of the eighteenth-century French architect Gabriel (the same goes for Blomfield's Central Library); others have described it as 'Potsdammer' style.

From the Usher you may retrace your steps back along Danes Terrace to the Jew's House, or may descend along the western side of Lindum Road and Broadgate to the river.

The line of the city wall lay to your right: the road is over the ditch. This way you will pass some fine early Victorian houses with iron balustrades near to the bottom of Lindum Road, while opposite is the former Sessions House, built as the city gaol from 1805. It is likely to become part of North Lincolnshire College. The former College of Art building of 1885 a short distance along Monks Road is again a part of that college. Across Monks Road is the Roman Catholic St Hugh's church (1893), recently cleaned and refurbished.

You are now at the city's busiest road junction.

You need to take care in crossing both Clasketgate (named after the medieval gate which stood here) and Silver Street, one of those streets which originated as a diagonal short cut in the early medieval period. You now come across the Constitutional Club, an attractive building of 1893 in serious need of cleaning, the castle-like Drill Hall of 1890, and finally the Greyfriars Museum. (The museum is due to be closed late in 1993 for a period of at least two and a half years to serve as the reference library, during construction work on the adjacent Lincoln Central Library. An alternative site is being actively sought.) The Greyfriars is dwarfed by the huge spire of St Swithin's church of 1870, inspired by the thirteenth-century gothic of the cathedral. The Victorian rebuild of the church, which contains a pagan Roman altar at the western end of its nave, involved a relocation from its medieval site in what is now a garden to the west, to the site of the former cattle market. Continuing south you reach the river by the Green Dragon Inn, an impressive jettied building much restored in the 1950s. Along the south side of the river to the east are some of the engineering factories of Clayton and Shuttleworth, and of Ruston Proctor, established in the 1840s and '50s.

That represents the noisier route down to the river but it does include a range of nineteenth-century buildings, some of them admittedly now rather grimy. Most walkers will wish to cling to the quieter, orthodox route which takes us southwards from the Jew's House down the Strait and on to High Street. At the narrow, southern end of the Strait is Dernstall House, a late fifteenth-century jettied building restored by Lincoln Civic Trust and formerly its headquarters.

You will arrive at the top of High Street back again on the line of the Roman Ermine Street, the main north–south artery of Lincoln's historical topography.

Looking up the aptly named Strait towards the cathedral

This upper part of the High Street tends to suffer commercially from being neither in the tourist area of uphill nor in the central shopping district further south, but attempts are being made at regeneration. To the west here lies St Martin's Square, the former site of one of Lincoln's most important early churches: the earliest local coinage was the St Martin penny of the 920s. Since its demolition, its graveyard has been laid out as a garden of rest, another amenity provided by the Lincoln Civic Trust.

Proceed southwards.

Here there are more structures of interest. On the right, Garmston House (Nos 262–3) is an early eighteenth-century building with Venetian windows. During its recent restoration, twelfth-century features were found in its north wall. Almost opposite, the half timbered Cardinal's Hat (No. 268) is of late fifteenth century: its name stems from the city's association with Cardinal Wolsey, dean and then bishop of Lincoln in 1509–14 before being called to higher office. It lies at the corner of Grantham Street (medieval Brancegate), which excavations showed had been laid out in the eleventh century to link a street (now Flaxengate) built in *c.* 900 with the High Street, whose medieval name was Mikelgate.

At the corner with Clasketgate is the former Boots store built in 1925. Construction work at cellar level revealed a Roman heating system, probably belonging to a public baths. When the cellar was converted to a public house and restaurant in the early 1980s, the surviving Roman fragment was incorporated into a mock-Classical interior with a peristyle and ceramic tiled fountain, and opened as 'The Roman Ruin'. Although this establishment has since closed, the interior remains, now as part of Charlie Mango's Rock Café, opened in September 1993.

Either proceed directly down High Street from the traffic lights to the Stonebow, or, if you are still feeling energetic, turn westwards along Corporation Street and West Parade until you reach the divisional police HQ on your right.

The building of 1973, known to some as 'Ryvita House' because of the rustic decoration of its concrete panels, is bounded on its far (western) side by the line of the western defences of the lower Roman city. They now lie buried (a small fragment is exposed as a marker), but the line is followed northwards by the cobbled pathway known as Motherby Hill and southwards by The Park: both were elements of Besome Park, a fashionable walkway created in 1720.

Turn south into The Park.

As you approach the concrete mass of City Hall (1973), note the well preserved rear face of the exposed Roman city wall on your right. All the masonry hereabouts belongs to a rebuilding of the mid-fourth century, including the gate whose tower bases incorporate some moulded and decorated fragments from an earlier classical temple or funerary monument.

Walk southwards a little way beneath the building and eastwards up the steps and on to the line of Park Street.

As you emerge into an open area, the Friends' Meeting House of 1689, an early example of a Quaker house, lies to your right at the south-west corner of the former graveyard (which originally belonged to a demolished nearby church). Continue in the same direction to the traffic lights on Newland, where the New Life Church (formerly

Congregationalist) of 1876 is on your right, its predecessor of 1840 adjacent. Further along and facing eastwards is a Victorian villa of 1880, now the headquarters of the Lincoln Labour Party.

Turn left towards the pedestrianized Guildhall Street – you may wish to go up Mint Street to have a quick look at the Baptist church of 1870, tastefully converted into an estate agent's office – along to the Stonebow.

The Stonebow is central Lincoln's principal meeting point, both in terms of modern rendezvous and because the City Council has met there for almost five hundred years. The Mote Bell of 1377 above summons the councillors to the meetings. The monument is mainly fifteenth century in date, although not finally completed until 1520 owing to a shortage of funds, but was considerably restored late last century. It lies on the site of the medieval city gate and, beneath that, its Roman predecessor. The Guildhall itself is above, and to the east the Mayor's Parlour. On the ground floor here are the Civic Insignia. They constitute an impressive collection of early documents – including the charter of 1157 – and artefacts, among them the Richard II sword and other items such as the Lincoln Race Cup. Guided tours are available at times.

Continue eastwards along Saltergate past the Still public house.

In the basement beneath the Royal Bank of Scotland are a section of the Roman south wall and a postern-gate, found in 1973. Guided tours are provided occasionally by staff of the museum. Past the neo-classical rear entrance of the Waterside Centre on the right, the Central Library and Greyfriars Museum are to the left, to the north of St Swithin's church. You may decide to visit these (but see note on p. 98).

Next turn right into Thorngate and arrive at the Green Dragon, where this tour rejoins the alternative route from the Usher Gallery. Then walk westwards along the riverside.

Part of the city's pedestrianized centre, with the new Waterside Centre (bottom right and centre), and the less loved designs of the 1950s and '60s (top right)

Your walk will now take you past another half-timbered building of early sixteenth-century date (its front is early nineteenth) also converted into a public house. The Witch and the Wardrobe was named after C.S. Lewis' children's story: it was formerly the A1 Fish Restaurant. Then you are upon the Waterside Shopping Centre, its southern façade a mixture of neo-classical and neo-medieval/Tudor. River trips leave from this point in summer. Across the river is the central market, its 1737 façade transferred here from the former Butter Market north of the Stonebow. To its left is Sincil Street, leading down to the other market areas: it probably lies over the line of the original Sincil Dyke at this point.

Looking westwards along the river, High Bridge and the half-timbered shops above are visible. As can be seen, some of the original bridge dates to the twelfth century – c. 1160 – with extensions to west and east. The sixteenth-century shops above were dismantled and rebuilt in 1900.

Cross the High Street and go down the steps to the right of the High Bridge into the so-called Glory Hole, whence a good view can be obtained of the bridge.

Continue along here – there *is* a continuous path in spite of the apparent obstacle in the form of a riverside brick building known locally as the Scout Hut. Eventually you will pass beneath Wigford Way to emerge at Brayford Head, where traffic used to pass over a swing bridge until its closure in 1972.

The Pool itself is an attractive, if dirty, space of water enhanced by the leisure craft moored here. The island acts as a home for some of its large population of swans. Its surroundings have lost what architectural integrity they had in the last twenty years or so, as almost all the surrounding mills and warehouses have been demolished – the last went in 1993 and only the Maltings and the 1898 electricity works offices on the north side remain. Their futures are in serious doubt. The replacement structures consist of an undistinguished and incompatible collection of offices and a multi-storey car-park, joined more recently by a large hotel in warehouse style. The worst offender must be the government office block at the western end of Brayford Wharf North: its northern frontage presents an even more undistinguished face on to Newland. I rate it below Wigford House on Brayford East, if only because I detect a redeeming feature in the latter's otherwise brutally intractable design. Its plan, with quasi-transepts, and its western face, six storeys high with horizontal bands of design can, with the eye of faith and seen from the south, be seen to reflect the horizontal zoning of the west front of the cathedral also in view – though I seem to be the only person in Lincoln to have noticed this and also to believe it.

Thus our hillside tour ends at the city's 'harbour', so busy last century with boats, but whose surrounding warehouses were unfortunately lost before it became fashionable to convert such buildings into residential units.

J.M.W. Turner's *Lincoln from Brayford*

3: The Wigford Walk

Our third trail will appeal particularly to those who have visited most of the attractions of the city centre to the north, or who wish to know more about the historical background of their locality. It covers the area from the Stonebow to South Common, along High Street: this was the important medieval suburb of Wigford (see Chapter Four) and also contained extensive suburban occupation and cemeteries in the Roman period. It now forms a mile long route with many shops, a number of important churches and chapels, and some interesting historic buildings. Most of the surviving structures date from no earlier than the eighteenth century, but there are some outstanding exceptions.

The walk starts at the Stonebow.

North and south of the Stonebow (itself described in walk 2) are two impressive banks, the National Westminster of 1883 (derived from the city's original Smith's Bank of *c*. 1775) and the Midland, roughly contemporary. Across from the Midland, little remains now of the Georgian Saracen's Head Hotel before you reach the mock-Tudor frontage of the Waterside Centre, which itself replaced a mock-Tudor Woolworths.

High Bridge has been mentioned in walk 2, but here note that there used to be a medieval chapel of St Thomas Becket on its eastern side. Early views of this area show the obelisk which replaced it, now also demolished.

From the south side of the river you can continue directly on towards St Benedict's church or take a detour to the left along Waterside South, past the C & A store to Sincil Street.

This alternative route provides a closer view of the Butter Market (now Central Market) frontage than was possible from across the river, and allows inspection of the markets area. Turn back westwards (to the right) again after the market stalls into Cornhill, past the newer Corn Exchange of 1879 on your right – the roof is worth seeing if you can gain access – and its predecessor, whose main part, in neo-classical style, was erected in 1847.

Between the Cornhill and the river, and behind the war memorial, is St Benedict's church, built originally after land reclamation in the twelfth century, although none of the existing fabric dates before early thirteenth. The squat tower, with Anglo-Saxon type openings, and its relationship to the nave – it appears to be later – would be most misleading, if you were not told that the nave had been so badly damaged in the Civil War that it was demolished and a new tower built against the chancel – which thus formed the new nave. Its windows are of some interest, too. Since it acts as a centre for the Mothers' Union, the church is normally open during the week.

On the south side of the square here is a new row of shops which replaced the former offices of the *Lincolnshire Echo* in similar style. At the corner, another bank, Lloyds, of *c*. 1900. There are also two impressive Victorian façades hereabouts – above the Dolcis shop opposite, and, further down, that of East Midlands Electricity (a William Watkins design), now cleaned and floodlit at night. The Cornhill itself was formerly the site of St John, one of Wigford's dozen or so medieval churches. Above Our Price Records is a fine fifteenth-century roof, which one day may be opened to public view.

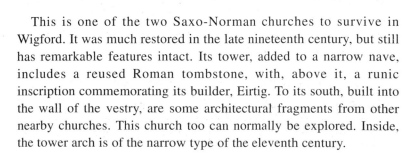

At the junction with St Mary's Street and Wigford Way, stay on the left (i.e. east) side as the pedestrian precinct comes to an end. Cross by the pedestrian crossing to St Mary le Wigford church.

The tall tower of St Mary le Wigford church, partially obscured by St Mary's Conduit

This is one of the two Saxo-Norman churches to survive in Wigford. It was much restored in the late nineteenth century, but still has remarkable features intact. Its tower, added to a narrow nave, includes a reused Roman tombstone, with, above it, a runic inscription commemorating its builder, Eirtig. To its south, built into the wall of the vestry, are some architectural fragments from other nearby churches. This church too can normally be explored. Inside, the tower arch is of the narrow type of the eleventh century.

In front of the church, on High Street, is St Mary's Conduit, built after the Reformation, probably from fragments of a fourteenth-century chapel at the Carmelite friary (beneath St Mark's railway station). Across the street here, beneath the Argos showrooms, was the site of late Iron Age finds, the earliest structures (first century BC/AD) found in the city so far.

We now cross the Great Northern Railway line of 1848 (the neo-Tudor station can be visited if you wish along St Mary's Street). It is easy to miss the next historic feature, which can be found down a passageway (Akrill's Passage) to the left; it is the southern, jettied elevation of a half timbered fifteenth-century building! The rest has gone, unfortunately.

Now continue down High Street, noting the lanes across the street which were a common feature: all led down to the Brayford Pool.

After the traffic lights, the former St Mark's church, whose site was excavated in 1976–7, has been replaced by a Kwiksave store. I find this comment on the late twentieth century amusing. Note the ground level is higher here, resulting from the displacement caused by the burial of hundreds of former parishioners.

On the east side here is a soulless modern block – the site of the former Sibthorp House, the townhouse of the leading family of the parish until they upped and left for nearby Canwick. The family vault was found in the excavations: one of the lead coffins had been inscribed 'Sibshorp' in error: we shall never know if the family was informed, or if they obtained a discount as a result.

As we reach the new magistrates courts on our left we are on the site of what used to be the High Street's other level crossing. The Midland Railway's station building of 1846 stands, rather decaying and forlorn, its Ionic portico supported by steel props, awaiting the implementation of a development scheme which will involve its restoration. (One has already received planning permission.) Excavations in 1986–7 between the platforms revealed Roman shops and part of the Carmelite friary, and on the east side, more Roman shops, a medieval house, and pottery and tile kilns of the fourteenth century. Another indication of the railway's presence is the kiosk on the south side of the court entrance: from here the crossing gates were controlled.

The magistrates' courts at St Mark's, built over the former Midland railway: the kiosk (right) controlled the crossing gates

Past the Ritz cinema/theatre, cross Portland Street by some Victorian houses.

The next buildings of note are Nonconformist chapels. Two are of historic interest: the small, early Georgian Unitarian chapel, with a later porch, and in contrast, the huge central Methodist church. As we cross Monson Street, note that this was where tombstones of Roman legionaries were discovered last century – some of the earliest information that a legion had been based in the city. But it is over a mile from the fortress, so had the tombstones been moved? Confirmation of the existence of a cemetery came in 1982, when several first-century cremation burials were uncovered beneath later Roman commercial buildings. By this point, it is possible that the two Roman roads running south have diverged, the Fosse Way continuing roughly on the line of the modern High Street, while Ermine Street heads off a little to the east. The evidence for this idea came from discoveries at Monson Street, where Roman buildings were discovered on a slightly different alignment from and well to the rear of the High Street. A street surface was also found at the eastern end of St Mary's Guildhall, which we now visit.

The Guildhall lies at the corner of Sibthorp Street, a street which was inserted at a later date, and early drawings show adjacent

Internal west wall of the restored west range of St Mary's Guildhall. Visible are a window (left), a partially rebuilt fireplace with 'joggled' stones and a blocked doorway (right). Beneath the carpet in the foreground the Roman Fosse Way is visible under glass panels

structures. To the rear here was also where Lincoln City Football Club played its first matches before moving to Sincil Bank in 1884. But the principal interest of St Mary's Guildhall is in the medieval and especially the Norman period. The possible context of the building's construction was described in Chapter Four. Civil War damage removed the southern part of the west range and its original roof has been much lowered, but the surviving detail indicates a palatial structure of *c.* 1150–70. The guild was certainly using the building in the thirteenth century, but the closest analogies to its design, which included also an early north range, are royal residences, and one suggestion is that it was built for Henry II's residence in 1157. In subsequent years its use was much altered, finally becoming a brewery and later a builders' depot. Most recently, the Lincoln Civic Trust took over responsibility for the building and completed the restoration of the west and south ranges several years ago, the former serving as its offices. The restored building is a pleasure to behold, both in terms of medieval and modern elements, as well as a section of Roman road (the Fosse Way) with wheel ruts visible beneath glass panels. The Norman building had encroached on to the road and used it as a foundation. Part of a Roman milestone was also found. Access to the interior is, however, restricted, and guided tours are only available on certain Saturdays during the year and for special events. An impression can at least be obtained from the street outside: the string course contains much variety.

There are other features of great interest in its vicinity. To the south, the other Saxo-Norman church, St Peter at Gowts, has an even more slender tower than St Mary's, although its door is a restoration. Again, a narrow nave adjoins it. There is also much of the thirteenth, fourteenth and nineteenth centuries. In front, by the pavement, is St Peter's Conduit, recently cleaned by the Lincoln Civic Trust. Across the street, an upstairs room at the Lincoln Arms public house contains a Norman arch, probably reset from St Andrews House, a fine Norman house which stood here till 1783. The adjacent row of cottages to the south could sit happily in a rural scene: they might date from as early as the seventeenth century.

Beyond this point, the walk becomes less rewarding, although the site of Gowts Bridge should be achieved. It carries Gowts Drain from the Witham to the west to Sincil Dyke to the east. The two watercourses helped drain the low lying land east and west of the High Street.

A further hike will bring the enthusiast to St Botolph's church.

108

The present building belongs mainly to the late nineteenth century, the tower being early Georgian, but these structures now betray little of the former grandeur of the medieval church, of cruciform plan, destroyed in the Civil War.

Not far beyond here was the medieval Bargate, and to its east, the Little Bargate. They were linked by a fragment of city wall, with the Sincil Drain outside.

Here we are on higher ground as South Common rises to the left. Roman legionary tombstones – including that of the Ninth Legion's standard bearer, Caius Valerius – and cremations have been found in the northern part of the Common. Their location has given rise to the idea that an early legionary base lies hereabouts, awaiting discovery. Also in this vicinity were the two medieval hospitals, including that of the lepers, and St Katherine's Priory: the large Victorian Methodist church sits on part of its site. Lincoln's Eleanor Cross was located here as the queen's body rested overnight in the priory chapel on the first stage of its journey from Harby, south-west of Lincoln, to London. A small fragment of the cross now remains in the grounds of Lincoln Castle.

If you want some breathing space, you can find it nearby on South Common, or alternatively at West Common, the Arboretum, Boultham Park or Hartsholme Country Park.

With that the tours are concluded.

Press). Both contain sections on the city.

With regard to original documents, the volumes published annually by the Lincoln Record Society have made a major contribution to the history of city and county. They include several important medieval collections, notably the *Registrum Antiquissimum* (several volumes edited by C.W. Foster and Kathleen Major), the Probate Inventories referred to in Chapter Six and edited by J.A. Johnston, and a bibliography of the city's history by D. Mary Short. A major history of the cathedral is imminent. The city's buildings are described in Nicholas Antram's revised edition of the Lincolnshire volume of the *Buildings of England* (Penguin Books, 1989). For more detailed accounts of houses, Lincoln Civic Trust's *Survey of Ancient Houses* series (three volumes to date; fourth in preparation) is covering both documentary and architectural evidence with exemplary scholarship and clarity. Archaeological discoveries meanwhile are covered briefly in Annual Reports, and in more detail in monographs, by the City of Lincoln Archaeology Unit. Some papers appear either in *Lincolnshire History and Archaeology* or in national journals.

Acknowledgements and Picture Credits

After several months' intermittent and sporadic information gathering, the writing of this book began in July 1993. It was drafted by early September. Summer is in many ways a good time to write, since the burden of administration tends to be less and academic libraries quiet. I benefited from both the calm and the resources of the libraries at Manchester University and Bishop Grosseteste College, Lincoln, where much of the hard reading was also carried out. With more tolerance than I deserve, my wife and family not only had to live with my absence at work during many evenings and several weekends, but also during our family holiday in western France, where the later sections were produced. My wife, Diana, also helped in the compilation of the index.

Mrs Greta Exton and her successor Mrs Angela Moore turned my drafts – necessarily in longhand – into neat typescripts. For advice on the medieval and later sections, I benefited from the expert knowledge of Dr Kathleen Major, Dr Jim Johnston, Neil Wright, Dr Dennis Mills and Keith Laidler. Inevitably, the book contains ideas derived from many sources, not all of which agree on interpretation or even date. Any errors which remain are entirely the fault of the author.

The following individuals and organizations have kindly allowed me to use many illustrations, without which the book would have been much poorer:

Aeroscan pages viii (upper), 20, 102; British Library page 55; British Museum page 2; C. Cruickshank and Heritage Lincolnshire pages 73, 74; European Gas Turbines and Mr R. Hooley page 71; C. Kerridge and Dr D. Mills page 72; *Lincolnshire Echo* and Peter Grey pages 62, 64, 76; Lincoln Cathedral Works Department pages 25, 54, and Fabric Fund Office 84; Lincoln City Council pages iv, viii (lower), ix, 4, 26, 42, 59, 69, 79, 81, 91 (upper), 106; Lincoln City Council Mayor's Office pages 29, 39; Lincolnshire County Council, Recreational Services: City and County Museum pages 3 (upper), 5, 88, Library Service pages 68, 75, Usher Gallery pages 53, 103, Tourism Section pages 21 (lower), 78, 91 (lower); Kevin Newton page 99; R. Sutton pages 14, 17, 18, 19; D.R. Vale pages 3 (lower), 6 (upper), 13, 21 (upper), 33, 49, 58, 61, 89.

The rest of the illustrations are from the collection of the City of Lincoln Archaeology Unit. The map for the walks was produced by Helen Palmer Brown and David Watt of the City of Lincoln Archaeology Unit, who were also responsible for several of the other drawings. The base for the map was provided by Rob Smith of Lincoln City Council (Department of Economic Development); he also gave much help with the photographs.

Index

The index lists only principal subjects and selected persons and places